ONE SIGNAL
PUBLISHERS

ATRIA

Also by Michael P. Murphy

The Architecture of Health:
Hospital Design and the Construction of Dignity

Justice Is Beauty: MASS Design Group (coauthor)

Empowering Architecture: The Butaro Hospital, Rwanda

OUR WORLD
IN TEN BUILDINGS

*How Architecture Defines
Who We Are and How We Live*

MICHAEL P. MURPHY

**ONE SIGNAL
PUBLISHERS**

ATRIA

New York   Amsterdam/Antwerp   London
Toronto   Sydney/Melbourne   New Delhi

ONE SIGNAL
PUBLISHERS

ATRIA

An Imprint of Simon & Schuster, LLC
1230 Avenue of the Americas
New York, NY 10020

First One Signal Publishers/Atria Books hardcover edition April 2026

ONE SIGNAL PUBLISHERS / ATRIA BOOKS
and colophon are registered trademarks of Simon & Schuster, LLC

Simon & Schuster strongly believes in freedom of expression and stands against censorship in all its forms. For more information, visit BooksBelong.com.

For information about special discounts for bulk purchases, please contact Simon & Schuster Special Sales at 1-866-506-1949 or business@simonandschuster.com.

The Simon & Schuster Speakers Bureau can bring authors to your live event. For more information or to book an event, contact the Simon & Schuster Speakers Bureau at 1-866-248-3049 or visit our website at www.simonspeakers.com.

Interior design by Davina Mock-Maniscalco

Manufactured in the United States of America

1 3 5 7 9 10 8 6 4 2

The Library of Congress Cataloging-in-Publication Data has been applied for.

ISBN 978-1-6680-5655-4
ISBN 978-1-6680-5657-8 (ebook)

Let's stay in touch! Scan here to get book recommendations, exclusive offers, and more delivered to your inbox.

This book is dedicated to Monique, Wilde, and Bobardi,
to whom I dedicate my life.

"What does architecture amount to
in the experience of the mass of men?
I never in all my walks came across a man
engaged in so simple and natural an occupation
as building his house. We belong to the community."

Henry David Thoreau, *Walden; or, Life in the Woods*, 1854

CONTENTS

CONTENTS

THE WAITING ROOM

International calls were expensive in 2005, especially those dialed into New York state from Cape Town, South Africa. They needed to be rare and short—but that would not stop my father and me from celebrating our birthdays that February, his fifty-third and my twenty-fifth.

My mother whispered as she answered. She and Dad were at the hospital. He had been feeling uncomfortable and wasn't eating. They went in to check it out, and the doctors opened him up to find that cancer was everywhere in his gut.

"They just sewed him back up," she said, her voice breaking. "They don't know how long. He might have only three weeks to live. When can you get home?"

"I'll leave tomorrow," I told her and dropped the phone. I had been traveling for a few months after burning out from my first job. I was trying to find a direction, but now all that was irrelevant. I had to get home.

Two international flights later—through Johannesburg and London—my brother Daniel picked me up at JFK in New York.

"How is he doing?" I asked, almost robotically.

"He comes home tonight. We're just waiting to hear more. A lot of people have been coming and leaving food and hoping to see him."

Dan, who is two years younger than me, had recently moved home after college in Chicago. He was waiting tables in town—and also waiting, as I was, to break the fever of our postgraduation ennui.

It was midwinter, and I was experiencing a whiplash back to the place where I so desperately tried to leave. The sky was bright blue, it was bitter cold, and the leaves were off the trees. I could see my breath as we walked to the car. I had missed that. The cool somber bite on my skin reminded me of my childhood. I felt an urge to kneel and kiss the ground.

Dan quickly got on the Taconic State Parkway, which starts in New York City—in the Bronx—and winds north to our hometown of Poughkeepsie, on the east bank of the Hudson River. We arrived at the house after two hours to find the front porch of the family home emptied of its furniture. The columns had been removed and the whole thing was propped up on cinderblocks, which meant the roof needed to be held up by wood planks jutting out into the yard around it. The place was always mid-renovation, as my father's never-ending punch list of home improvement projects never finished.

For as long as I could remember, on Saturdays I'd watch him throw on a paint-flecked sweatshirt from our high school crew team to practice his therapy of home renovation. My parents had bought the house fifteen years earlier, desirable for its price—still a financial stretch for us—but in need of a lot of work. It was not in the most desirable location, but it was close to school, big enough for the brood, and near enough to both their jobs to make it work for the family. The unique Victorian home, with period details and historic characteristics, had been purchased draped in layers of old lead paint that needed remediation. The roof (and windows) leaked and had to go, too. The kitchen would be remodeled, and the entire third floor was unfinished and raw.

Instead of hiring a contractor, my father and mother wanted to save money and do it themselves. The result was a slow, endless renovation. Each year, my father had one or two major projects he did on Saturdays. He was in no rush. Usually, it was painting. He wanted to hand-strip every layer of old paint from the clapboards and then repaint them. He spent an entire summer stripping one side of the house and then the fall repainting it.

But I don't know if he ever meant to finish. He and the house were in a fused state of repair and re-repair.

Dad's meticulousness taught me that any project is doable—and big projects, while they might take years, were accomplished iteratively, one brushstroke at a time. A lesson that would come in handy as I leaned into larger projects later in my career. At the pace he kept on the house, he must not have thought too much about his own mortality. But now the doctors sobered him up—he might have only three weeks to live. They told us he could go home from the hospital to be with his family and settle his affairs.

———

Dan and I were the first to arrive that evening, getting a chance to survey the home on our own for a moment. It was, frankly, in a state of disrepair. It reminded me how much none of us had planned for this. Suddenly, Dan and I took on the personality of the house, entering a state of extended limbo, awaiting some form of miracle.

The living room was dark and cold, the thermostat at 60 degrees. The cost of heating an old drafty house kept us in sweaters and hats while indoors. They had been alone in a big house, huddling in just a few rooms. The house smelled like the fireplace had been recently used. Things were stacked everywhere—boxes of wine and platters of neighbor-donated meals in the pantry—and a huge Entenmann's coffee cake was sitting untouched on the kitchen island.

We'd always spent much of our time there, in that kitchen, one of four rooms that made up the downstairs floor plan. The layout of the house was rectangular with the living room and den on opposite sides at the front of the house and the kitchen and dining room opposite each other at the back of the house.

I sat down on the den chair where Dad usually sat and looked at the bookshelves piled with political tomes and slow historical books. A survey of his other meditation. Like his housework, he addressed these goliaths as projects to be conquered and kept a running tally in his yellow legal pads of which books he was reading each quarter and how many pages he read per night. When I weighed reading his favorite book the summer before, Robert Caro's *The Power Broker*, about New York City's infrastructure pharaoh Robert Moses (clocking in at 1,246 pages), he presented a simple equation to assuage me. "Fifty pages a night, you will finish it in less than a month. No sweat," he said. To my father, anything was achievable with a system that foresaw its completion. That is, until now.

Sitting there, I recognized on the shelf a left-behind book of mine covered in a red cloth jacket. It was my copy of Henry David Thoreau's *Walden*, received as a high school graduation gift from my uncle Mike Knipfing. I had read it that first summer after school. My father must have rescued it from my piles of books upstairs and placed it on the more presentable living room shelves he had built. I pulled it down and started thumbing through the parts I had underlined:

> I went to the woods because I wished to live deliberately. To front only the essential facts of life and see if I could not learn what it had to teach, and not, when I came to die, discover that I had not lived.

Prophetic words in 1854, as Thoreau stripped his life down to the essentials of life, if only as a means of seeing more clearly. He separated himself from his community and moved alone to the woods around Walden Pond in Concord, Massachusetts. To survive there, Thoreau's first act was to build a shelter, and so *Walden* becomes as much a meditation on the home as fundamental to survival as it does on survival itself. Thoreau investigates the materials with which we construct our homes and how they represent and reflect the identity of the "indweller," their inhabitant.

Thoreau died from tuberculosis in 1862, less than ten years after the publication of *Walden*. Throughout he ponders his legacy. Thoreau writes that he wants to learn life's lessons "And not, when I came to die, discover that I had not lived." I wondered about Dad's legacy. Did he think that his was a life well lived? What proof did he have? I came to realize that his legacy, all the proof he needed, was all around me in the way he repaired and restored our home.

I wondered if this house was exhausting my dad, working on it tirelessly in all his off-hours. His whole life seemed to be made up of the paint on the walls and on the clapboard siding. I wondered if I could help lift this endless burden and do something, anything to keep my mind busy in this purgatory, this endless waiting room.

That night, Dad came home from the hospital and immediately poured himself a drink, sat in his chair, and turned on CNN. I was sitting near him on the couch. It was around 6 p.m.

"Are you going to die?" I asked him.

"Not if I have anything to do about it," he said, unfazed by the challenge ahead. "I'm going to fight."

After some time there was a commercial break.

"What are you going to do with this place?" I asked him.

"I am finishing it," he said, without missing a beat.

"What would it mean to complete this house?" I asked.

He looked at me, staring through me, to the end of the tunnel. "Well, you know the third floor has never been touched," he said. Then a list popped into his mind. "We need to finish that to make a little more room. Down here, I'd like to spruce up the living room. It's a bit of a puzzle why some of these spaces are the way they are. In the spring, I want to replace the front porch and finish painting the exterior clapboard. We need a new roof next year. Then it will be closer to finished."

He spoke as if he intended to live forever.

Chapter 1

THE HOME

Poughkeepsie, New York

W hat was this space originally designed to be?" I asked my dad upstairs, perplexed by the unfinished third floor of the Murphy family homestead. "Do you know anything about the architect? Do you have a sense of what we are restoring it to?"

"I have no idea. It was built, I think, around 1896. They cared about this place, though. It has good bones."

Dad was beginning an aggressive chemo regime, so we were entering a state of wait-and-see. Nonetheless, that next morning, he went back to work. To keep my mind distracted, I decided to chase Dad's curiosity and take up the herculean task of exhuming the house's history—if only to get a sense of where to begin. My first stop would be downtown at the county office building.

It held all the deeds and documents of the city's properties. The ground floor was the Department of Motor Vehicles, taxes on floor two, and property on three. Dad worked in the building on the fifth floor, where the county executive's office was who he worked for. Long, table-height bins filled with files gridded the third floor, a few people hunched over searching through them.

I caught someone's attention and asked how I might search for the history of my house on Dwight Street. The person gave me a wide-eyed "what-are-you-doing-here" look and introduced herself as Jennifer Clum. "I was your old babysitter when you were little!" Jenn said. "We were just thinking about your dad. How is he?" she asked with a pause.

Jenn toured me through the long archival threads that linked each property together, and we found the original title document of our house. It was written in cursive with a fountain pen. The listed owner was a woman named Mary Howell, and she had inherited the land from J. O. Whitehouse, her father. Jenn also found an old development plan for our neighborhood before its houses were even built. Whitehouse's estate had been separated into about sixty plots for future construction. Ours and four others were mapped out as the first to be built. On the lower-right corner of the plan was the line *Horace Trumbauer, Architect, July 1896.* I left with printouts and replicas of the original street plan, but most importantly, I had the name of the person who designed our house.

Searching for Trumbauer online revealed a trove of information and completed buildings. He had designed grand estates of the newly rich of Philadelphia in the 1920s and 1930s. He had built grand cultural institutions like the Philadelphia Art Museum (where Rocky ended his famous stair run) and one of his most prestigious commissions, the Widener Library at Harvard University—the centerpiece of Harvard Yard. Look at that, a famous architect had designed our home, and no one knew it.

Trumbauer's archives were held at the Athenaeum of Philadelphia. I called them the next day to get some help on where to start, and while they had no plans of our house, they pointed me to an early influence on his work, that of Frank Lloyd Wright's first commissions in Oak Park, Illinois. In 1895, Frank Lloyd Wright had designed the

Nathan G. Moore House in Oak Park, a suburb of Chicago where he lived and worked. It had an eccentric mix of shapes, different roof types, and asymmetric forms. The house had strong triangular gables, angled church-like windows, and used the long, flat, prairie-style bricks that were later seen in his groundbreaking Robie House in the Hyde Park neighborhood of Chicago. I had walked by the Robie House every day during college on my way to class and long admired its horizontal lines and volumetric shapes. I often remarked how contemporary and stylistically modern it looked even though it was older than many structures around it, built in 1906. It felt out of time. The Moore House was different though, and eclectic—like a bricolage of varying voices fighting for airtime. Wright experimented with a range of materials and shapes with the Moore House, and the outcome was a collage of architectural ideas—some of which he would keep and some he would discard. It looked like a grander, more expensive version of our Trumbauer-designed house in Poughkeepsie.

As I embarked on this journey, I imagined Horace Trumbauer scouring publications of buildings from that era and finding inspiration from the young Wright for our home. The chimney at the Moore House was a soaring wall shooting through the roof like a razor blade, signaling to the world around it that the house was divided into two halves. In our home, the mantel over the fireplace was festooned with fleur-de-lis carvings. It was grand and ornate and certainly ostentatious for my parents' humble tastes.

They didn't have the money to build their own home, let alone live in the one we had in its heydey. It'd been a bargain stowed away in Poughkeepsie after the moneyed class and industry abandoned it in the middle of the twentieth century.

When my parents bought it, the third floor was dark and dingy with cheap wall-to-wall carpeting and wood paneling from the 1970s that made it unusable for anything other than storage. The four rooms were filled with boxes, old furniture, junk, and books in piles. I went upstairs with a hammer and box cutter to make a mess.

One trait I picked up from my father is the ability to sit in any room, no matter what is happening around me, and read. Even though I made my mess on the third floor by day, at night I started pulling books from shelves and learning about architecture.

The word *architecture* is from the Latin *architectura* and has two primary definitions. The first is "the art and practice of designing and constructing buildings," and that makes sense, because it is about making buildings. The second definition of *architecture* is "the structure of things," like the chemical architecture of wood fibers. I liked that dual meaning, that architecture could refer to the minuscule invisible structure of materials as well as the very visible and inhabitable structures throughout our world. Architecture is all around us and in everything we touch.

The first real theorist of architecture was a Roman builder named Vitruvius. He said that "the ideal building has three elements; it is sturdy (*firmitas*), it is useful (*utilitas*) and it is beautiful (*venustas*)."

For something to be sturdy made sense to me. Thoreau knew that if he hoped to immerse fully in nature, his first act was to build a basic shelter. Even the simplest hut of wood and mud creates a shield from the natural elements of a place. If shelter is in a tropical climate, it has to face heavy winds and rain but also moisture and heat. If it is in the northeast of the United States, like my family's house or Henry Thoreau's cabin in the woods, the roof has to support snow from a long winter and have a fireplace to keep inhabitants warm during cold nights.

This is where the architect becomes an engineer, solving for essential sheltering responsibilities in the context where it exists. The sturdiness of a thing, the "good bones" my dad pridefully mentioned our house had, made instant sense to me. To be sturdy, to have *firmitas*, was to stand up, protect, and keep whoever was inside comfortable, regardless of the climate around them.

My eyes were opened even more to the idea that a place could offer many uses, more than simple protection. Architects call these uses the "programs" of the space— places to sleep, eat, rest, store our things, entertain our friends, and live much of our lives. And often the first act of architecture is to determine how much space is needed for those uses now and in the future. Too much space can be excessive, expensive, and useless—but too little can feel cramped and poorly planned. As a family adds children and elderly parents, or shrinks as children leave and the nest empties, this balance of usefulness changes. A well-designed house anticipates—it remains useful as it evolves, by being adaptable to the evolving needs of its inhabitants.

In addition to our downstairs, our house had four bedrooms on the second floor, a grand porch, and a basement for storage. These were all used as intended. The kitchen, however, was used differently than it was designed. It was small and closed off from the rest of the house and was accessed through a single door. Today in houses we see open plans of kitchens that blend into living rooms, but old houses closed off rooms to protect heat and to separate the spaces used for making the food from ones where the food was eaten. We still crowded ourselves around the kitchen island to surround my mother as she cooked, but changing the physical structure of the home to make this perhaps easier—an open plan, as it is called today—wasn't practical. We adapted to it and it to us by squeezing more chairs around the island and putting a second fridge in the basement. It felt crowded and compact but full of life and energy.

An architect has to be a kind of fortune teller. Programming a house is about stress testing its limits to reveal how the house will function effectively and pleasantly in the future, despite who it was designed for. Every home contains little tells or insights about a family's behavior to inform this. A hospital bed in the living room would suggest stairs may be too difficult to manage and aging in place might need to happen elsewhere. A pile of wine boxes on the floor might suggest the need for more storage (to which Frank Lloyd Wright would likely object, insisting on having *less stuff* as the answer to most things). If all your children move home after an illness and the empty nest feels crowded again, renovating the attic might release some built-up pressure. When my dad came home from the hospital, our family stress tested the home anew, and Dad and I set to work customizing the space for this new normal.

———

Back upstairs I ripped off the paneling in one of the third-floor rooms. The nails came out easily, bringing old plaster with them and creating clouds of dust. I found ancient floral wallpaper underneath that was covering a plaster wall. Holes revealed wood lath and the framing structure beyond. Someone had once attempted to strip off the wallpaper as it was ripped in many places—I wondered if the pieces still hanging on had been left by Mary Howell herself. They were torn and stained from water damage.

The doorframe had children's scribbles, recording their heights.

Thomas, 2'8"

Margaret was here

Adam, 3'5" 1970

Surely no one else had seen these markings in decades. I created a pile in the center of the room as I ripped down layer after layer, revealing the many hands of the long relay race of stewards who had held this place together before me.

Stripped down to its essentials, I saw how small and dark the room was. I was inspired to break through the wall to the next room and connect it with glass doors like the ones in the living room below. My other uncle Mike, my father's brother by marriage, was a carpenter, and he said the wall was not structural, so we could knock through it, squeeze in a wood doorframe, and find an old French door from a salvage place he knew up the river. He showed me some carpentry tips and instructed me on fastening drywall panels to ceiling and walls, taping the seams, and covering them with joint compound.

Dad came home from work in astonishment to see the reframed third floor open and new. I imagined his chair in the new sunlit room and us sitting there in silence.

"It's been five weeks," he said. "I'm still here."

I had forgotten all about the deadline.

"Well, block out some time," I told him. "We are ready to paint."

Now I was an adult, and I was picking up my father's paint brush. I was making this house my own.

The architect's third responsibility, beyond being an engineer or a social scientist, is its highest and most difficult achievement—to design spaces that are so beautiful they become art forms in their own right. As simple as applying a coat of paint or refinishing a surface, it can do so much to visually reawaken the latent beauty of a space.

As I bonded with the physicality of the house, through stripping and sanding and refinishing, I began to intimately understand how it all came together. This wasn't merely a box full of people, and it wasn't the drawings and schematics I'd make a living creating later in my life. It was a joining of crafted materials used to create that visual composition of paint and wood, window and wall. I came to think about the craftsmen who spent weeks making the wood trim or the stained-glass window, and the love and care they put into their work. I imagined workers' hands on all the surfaces that I was now touching and felt a connection across time and space. I felt bound to this place and to the people who built it.

Dad started coming home early from work to get in a few hours of painting before dinner, and I was happy to oblige. He loved the meticulousness and certainty of the task. He bought a small quart of silver paint, which he used to touch up the radiators and suddenly these rusty old beasts popped with reflective sheen. We bled them out for the first time in perhaps thirty years. For the floor trim, he insisted we use Benjamin Moore's eggshell white.

He lay on his side on the wooden floor in the third-floor hallway, propped up on his elbow, with a small paintbrush in his left hand. Without taping, without a cloth to protect the floor, he painted the trim perfectly with no drips. He was comfortable thinking through the moves on the chessboard left to him, and he did so without equivocation.

From his spot on the floor, he asked me, "What do you think you're going to do, Michael?"

I was busy rolling primer paint on the wall—a task that required much less precision.

"I left everything behind in South Africa," I said, not knowing what exactly that was. "I thought I wanted to be a writer, a journalist maybe, but I had to come home to be with you."

"I did not want you to come home for me," he said. "Your life is more important. You can't wait for me. What do you think you'll do?"

In the weeks since my birthday, in the time I'd been working in that old attic space, I felt as if I had been reborn. I was not incrementally growing but instead transported forward in a singular burst into a new shell of adulthood.

"I don't know, Dad," I said. "You know, this work with you, this house. I like it. It is nice to see the change. I wonder if I might want to study architecture."

My father hardened himself and looked me in the eye. "I think that is a wonderful idea."

———

By May, as the seasons changed, so did our house. The third floor was finished, and I moved my bedroom up there. It felt different to sleep in the room instead of work on it. I was proud of it, and after touching almost every square inch of its surfaces, the space felt like it was truly mine, even though it had had many owners over its 110 years of life.

I saw the house evolve when we toiled to make it so. Remaking the house left evidence of our own existence in the world. My father wanted to leave something behind for us, and he wanted to see the change he desired actualized in the real world. He wanted to recognize that he restored it himself and know it would not have happened without him. The building was his legacy.

Restoring the third floor during that winter, I realized, filled an unconscious need to avoid facing my father's imminent death. I focused on what little my hands could do and on the small world I could control. Maybe I was tuning into what Thoreau had found at Walden Pond, what he called "the unconscious beauty of life." Thoreau continues:

"What of architectural beauty I now see, I know has gradually grown from within outward, out of the necessities and character of the indweller, who is the only builder—out of some unconscious truthfulness, and nobleness, without ever a thought for the appearance and whatever additional beauty of this kind is destined to be produced will be preceded by a like unconscious beauty of life."

I started to plot the rest of the projects on my father's list. Next was the living room, and when the weather warmed, the outside tasks like the porch, finishing the clapboard painting, and finally fixing the leaking roof.

———

What makes a house into a home? The home is not so much a singular place as it is an emotional experience that only a place can elicit. Home is the projection of that feeling, and even an existential condition, where our minds begin to shape elemental relationships. The philosopher Gaston Bachelard in his book *The Poetics of Space* argued that the house "shelters daydreaming" and so provides the foundation of all image-making in the mind. He says that the house "is one of the greatest powers of integration for the thoughts, memories, and dreams of mankind ... It is body and soul. It is the human being's first world." Neuroscientists have begun to study these phenomenological conditions and people's reflection of them.

Dr. Anjan Chatterjee, a neuroscientist at the University of Pennsylvania, has explored this sensation, the feeling of "hominess" in our consciousness. Through his work, Chatterjee has found that the human brain responds to aesthetic compositions such as symmetry, balance, rhythm, and color in ways that show consistent physiological responses across cultures, in ways that demonstrate how architectural aesthetics trigger pleasure receptors in our brains.

Chatterjee has argued that even though contexts vary, that sense of "home" is universal and is elemental to the human mind. The brain seeks comfort in this feeling, strives to re-create it, and is attracted to spaces that draw it out in us. This attraction leads us to pursue aesthetic choices to elicit that warm feeling in the spaces we frequent throughout life, to search for the hominess in the world around us. The mind craves security, and no other space elicits the deeply hardwired emotions of nostalgia and comfort, memory and consciousness like our homes.

Three weeks turned into eighteen months. As the seasons progressed and the calendar turned over, Dad carried on. There he was, more often than not, standing guard out front of the house, still in his paint-stained shirt, holding his glass of Canadian Club and Diet

Coke. The doctors told us he was in remission and his outcome unclear. While stage four cancer is, for all intents and purposes, a death sentence, Dad's future was hopeful. "I love standing here at the end of the day admiring what we've done," he told me. It was his favorite thing to do, seeing the changes and planning what was next.

"Working on this house with you, Michael—it saved my life."

I thought just possibly it had also saved mine.

———

Something deeper must be at play here. These homes, we shape them and they shape us; but to my father, this house also provided him with something deeper, the fuel to survive, the purpose to keep going, an existential grace. As the home was revived, he too was restored, and I was given a window into the role these buildings can play for each of us, no matter our lot in life, as a purveyor of hope in physical form.

Down the street, other families also began restorations on their homes. They were taking seriously the historic nature of this street, and one of the neighbors applied to put the street on the state and national register.

In blocks surrounding us in Poughkeepsie, more and more families were taking pride in their own homes and starting to renovate them. It felt like a renaissance, and I became hopeful that change and health and possibility were in front of us. Could this beat-up old town get off life support and start its own remission? What life forces gave us the will to live? Were these inspirations in spaces all around us? I could feel my mind opening. I started to see the world differently. I now saw voices, hands, legacies in the trim and the plaster and the polished door handles around me. I knew then what I needed to do. I needed to become an architect.

Chapter 2

THE SCHOOL

Cambridge, Massachusetts

I arrived at architecture school naïve to the world I was about to enter. I was in exile from Poughkeepsie, fresh off the longer leash my father was on from his cancer screening. I had one foot in the new and the other stuck firmly at home. So I rushed through the building trying to hide all that baggage to find my desk.

Harvard's Graduate School of Design is a monster. The building it's headquartered in—Gund Hall—was named after its benefactor, George Gund II, a man who made his fortune off decaffeinated coffee, a substance that appeared, by my observation, to rarely if ever be drunk in this building. Gund Hall sat on the corner of a busy intersection, with large concrete columns and a deep-set entrance located underneath the building above. Across the street was (what looked like) a large Gothic cathedral, if going by its statues and detailing, though in reality it housed a dining hall, a hub of classrooms, a theater, and a student center. Gund Hall was stark, brutalist architecture, with lifting forms and long shadows. Both buildings felt old, but of different eras. They lied about their age. On the wall was a plaque with the inscription "Graduate School of Design, Harvard, John Andrews, Architect, 1972."

The entrance to the GSD was cold and compressed. The lobby, if you can call it that, is really a hallway. Concrete walls were used as a gallery of sorts, and models sat atop wooden podiums throughout the corridor space. The darkness ricocheted around the spotlit panels that were covered in printed boards with text, images, and three-dimensional representations of buildings.

The interior space begged for light. Only glass doors on either side of the hallway—one in direct sight and one off in a corner—allowed the sun's relief. The entrance loomed and intimidated, creating a space I felt I didn't belong in.

A set of propped-open double doors let the light pour in and beckoned me through to a staircase. At the landing that turned my body 180 degrees, I soaked in the full view above of five open stories. There were no columns breaking up the view of dozens of desks where architecture students sat drawing, modeling, and computing away on their designs. It was a hive. With the swirl of anxiety and the intimidation of excellence, I realized this was the new world.

Gund was unlike any building I had experienced before. Each floor seemed to slide past the one below it, leaving all five floors open to the light-filtered ceiling soaring above them. These were the "trays." The building resembled a staircase for a giant. And giants of our field—we were sure to be reminded—had filled these floors before us.

The floors were set up—intentionally or not—to reproduce that hierarchy. Older classes were at higher trays. Second years on the third tray, third years on the fourth, and thesis students in the final year, at the fifth tray, looking down upon the entire school, talking and fomenting work over the semester. The very nature of our orientation to this setup was perplexing. We were to spend these years sweating it out among one another. Only some would succeed.

There was nowhere to hide, and everyone would be on full display and under the judgment of all who'd come before us.

My studio was on the second tray, a floor up from the mezzanine with desks huddled toward the banister and clustered in groups of four. A "Studio," in architecture school parlance, is a cluster of twelve to fifteen students and one faculty member. This would be my cohort—my tribe—for the entire first semester of school.

Studio was all-consuming; it was everything we were supposed to think about and care about. All-nighters were expected from students. I would regularly arrive at 7 a.m. and leave at 2 a.m. Our apartments were messy bedrooms, with unused couches and fridges full of desiccating condiments. Every meal, every coffee, every conversation happened at Gund, as we collectively immersed ourselves through adaptation and submission. It was a pressure-cooker culture of expectation and production.

————

Our first instructor was a charismatic storyteller named T. Kelly Wilson, who expected us to arrive each day with a set of pencils with different lead weights and thicknesses. Wilson wanted us to learn architectural drawing as they learned in the Beaux-Arts de Paris in the nineteenth century—the foundational school for architectural education. The basics start with how a building is drawn on paper and represented. There are three major drawings that show a building in two dimensions: the plan, the section, and the elevation.

The plan is the most common and familiar: a two-dimensional drawing of a building's floor plan, showing the rooms divided by walls, each measured proportionally using a scale ruler. Andrea Palladio (1508–1580) was one of the most revered draftsmen at the twilight of the Italian Renaissance. His plans, elevations, and sections show how a simple drawing can communicate a complex structure, as in the following image.

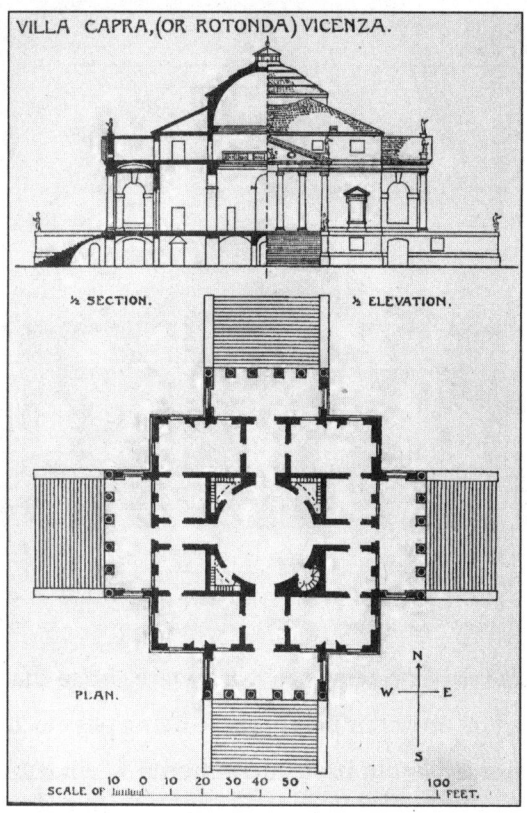

An elevation is a two-dimensional drawing of a building's façade, from the outside, showing windows and siding and general form. Elevation drawings can be odd to the uninitiated because they do not show perspective or depth. They are flat, two-dimensional, meant to show exact measurable relationships between elements like the windows and their frames and the distance to the ground.

The third is the section drawing, which is like the elevation but taking the façade off so we can see inside the building from floor to floor—like in a dollhouse. A plan, a section, and an elevation are all orthographic drawings—ways to represent three-dimensional objects in two dimensions. An architect, Wilson told us, can describe almost any building this way. Another Palladio example, here, to illustrate a section:

The next set of drawings to learn were those that show three dimensions. The most familiar of these being perspective drawings, which many of us would have encountered when learning to draw in grade school.

———

Perspective drawing is about how the eye sees the world. These drawings, unlike plans, sections, or elevations, are not measurable drawings. A builder cannot use them to calculate distances and construct from them. For that there is the axonometric drawing. These were more complicated but use the same mathematical principle, called *projection*, to show measurable drawings in three dimensions.

The most familiar example, perhaps, comes from a failed

architecture student. Haarlem School of Architecture and Decorative Arts alum (but not architecture graduate) M. C. Escher drew the famous Penrose staircase, which used the principles of geometric drawing to create illusions and improbable conditions.

This was how all architects had been taught to design since the Renaissance. Learn to draw buildings in these simple ways and almost anything can follow. However, the act of drawing by hand was being phased out as computer modeling and computational architecture were taking over coursework, the world of construction, and the trays themselves. Mine would be the last class of its kind to train our hands to put ideas to paper.

The first assignment we were asked to design was an updated cabin for Henry David Thoreau on Walden Pond. I was surprised by this assignment. What were the chances that one of my foundational texts would be my first entry to design? I had the impression I had imagined this place in my mind for so long that the sheer coincidence of the assignment felt like a sign. Maybe I was not as unprepared as I felt, I pondered a little too opportunistically.

Walden Pond was close, about fifteen miles away from the GSD, in Concord, Massachusetts. We were told it was up to us to interpret the makeup of the architecture and were asked to draw a plan, a section, an elevation, and perspectives.

———

For my first building, dozens of questions related to proportion and relationships suddenly flooded my head. I knew so little about how things went together. How high should a railing be, or what is a reasonable width of a hallway, or the height of a door? Professor Wilson encouraged us to learn from our building itself, instead of looking it up in a standards book or online, and respond to the spaces as we felt them. And sure enough, Gund Hall itself had functioned as its own teaching tool, a heuristic about size, proportions, standard measurements, and replicable conditions we might model our own drawings on.

For instance, to determine what a "normal" width of a hallway might be, or how wide a public staircase should be made, Gund provided an easy answer. On the floor were twelve-inch tile coverings, so when I looked down, I could count one, two, three, four tiles, four feet, as a reasonable width of a hallway without pulling out a measuring tape or consulting a code reference book. Same with the stairs, six tiles wide and one tile deep, but not a full tile high.

In front of my desk on the trays was one of two staircases that climbed the entirety of the building, open, on display, crossing the "trays." It was a visible and clear lesson about how a building functioned using standard dimensions of industrialized construction products, and what it looked like when those standards were adjusted for the needs of the people using it.

My design for *Walden* was more a treehouse than a cabin, perched on the hillside on thin columns with a diamond-shaped floor plan and a wraparound deck to look out over the pond. I covered it with a roof design inspired by Thoreau's quote, "A man has no more to do with the style of architecture of his house than a tortoise with that of its shell." I turned my effort toward drawing an extreme perspective that showed the porch railing looking like a precipice and taped together sheets of paper to demonstrate how the final form would meet the extents of the building's roofline.

I brought my red-covered text to the review and read quotes from *Walden* in the presentation, seeking shelter behind my English lit education. The reaction from the faculty was less optimistic. They could see past the crutch I was holding and pinpoint the illogical misfires in the design. Why was the structure perched so high, on such fragile and thin columns? The bathroom's location destroyed the floor plan and would be impossible to use. And then the fatal blow came when the instructor asked if the glass-and-steel construction was antithetical to Thoreau's environmentalist ethos, and shouldn't these material choices be more—of the place?

I rolled up my drawings and walked out deflated and demoralized. It was true. I had tried to tackle something I thought I knew intimately, but I had missed the signs popping off the page in front of me. I had to learn to read differently, like an architect.

We did not know how much we, as students, were on our own precipice in the field. Half the reason Kelly was insistent on starting us at drawing was just how far the technological revolution had already transformed the way our colleagues and industry were being perceived and the roles we could play. It was 2006, the penultimate year before the financial collapse of the Great Recession, where among the first jobs to go would be those of architects.

But at this time, the world still felt ascendent. It was the apex of the "starchitect" era in architecture, when architects took on mythic, heroic status as they collected international accolades. We were not yet fully engaged in the social media age, but that instinct for celebrity and notoriety had arrived early.

At the time, Frank Gehry was the most famous architect alive because of his swoopy, reflective Guggenheim Museum in Bilbao, Spain (ca. 1997), which shocked the world for its bold forms that looked like crumpled paper emerging as flames from the ground.

His museum was sculptural and formally arresting from the outside. Inside were spaces with tilting walls and galleries of unfamiliar shapes. All this was made possible by the adaptation of computer programs designed for aerospace to architectural form finding, which Gehry trailblazed. "Bilbao"—as we referred to it—was a new era of formally bold buildings, and a race to construct forms that would have been nearly impossible to draw by hand in architecture just a few years prior.

Gehry's work was visually stunning and an enormous feat architecturally, and it was also credited with transforming the city of its placement. Bilbao was an industrial outpost that had seen economic decline, but after the Guggenheim it was an art and culture destination. This was an undeniable justification of the value of architecture, many argued. It was an example that great buildings could enhance positive economic and cultural change for a place. Architecture was a discipline of dreams and promise. City leaders around the world wanted their own "Bilbao" revitalizations, and design schools shifted their pedagogical capacities to fulfill that potential.

In school, this translated to that shift in the debate of how great architecture was made. In one way, the new tools were democratizing, increasing in speed and iteration the possibilities hand drawing restricted; on the other hand, the technology could obscure projects that were not conceptually rigorous.

Strength, utility, and beauty, as Vitruvius had laid out, still made sense; however, debate at the school was reconsidering those principles' relative worth. If beautiful and sculptural architecture could revitalize a place, we should all be aiming to make the next Bilbao. *Venustas* (beauty) was overtaking *utilitas* (utility) and *firmitas* (strength).

In fact, a nineteenth-century architect named Louis Sullivan had engaged in this debate once before. In his time the Industrial Revolution had brought a new wave of industrial building materials and forms, and Sullivan, one of America's first modern architects, dove in. He was the "father of skyscrapers," innovative for his use of steel frames over masonry that allowed humankind to build higher and larger buildings. The core structures were stronger and could now expand vertically to meet the needs of population-dense cities and the emergent businesses growing within them. America was diverging from European trends of low-rise building and ushering in new formal expressions and architectural theories in what we now call "the modern era" (after 1910). Sullivan theorized that the skyscraper epitomized something about this new time, encapsulated by his famous maxim "Form follows function," which he justified as a natural phenomenon:

> It is the pervading law of all things organic and inorganic, of all things physical and metaphysical, of all things human and all things superhuman, of all true manifestations of the head, of the heart, of the soul, that the life is recognizable in its expression, that form ever follows function.

Having form follow function meant that a building's shape, configuration, character, and even its symbolism were second to—or responded to—how it needed to perform. What were the uses of the building and how would it stand in its climate needed to be solved first, and the form of it, the large skyscraper in this case, would fill a city block because the function—its corporate office tenants—required it to.

This maxim defined modern architecture for the next century. But with starchitecture at its apex in the aughts, and computer-aided tech emerging alongside new building trends, the maxim had been reversed—function was now following form.

Some influential architects even argued that a building's functionality—its utility and strength—were insignificant when compared to the artistic achievement that was possible in architecture. What Gehry proved with his museum in Bilbao and later with his Disney Concert Hall in Los Angeles is that with these new tools, even the impossibly complex and undrawable could now be built easily. It was a watershed moment and ushered in a new era of Formalism, when the building's form, its artistry, its sculptural properties, its aesthetics and beauty quotient, heralded over all others.

We were told to think of architecture as a Venn diagram where one circle is engineering (strength), one is social science (utility), and the other is form (beauty or artistry). Formalism placed architecture much further into artistry, because suddenly technology—computational technology—allowed for the impossible mathematics of avant-garde engineering to become buildable and realizable. This fusing of technology and form-making transformed the buildings in the world around us and thus the discipline itself—the schools—were playing catch-up. If the computer can figure out the calculations, there is no need to really understand that part of building. There would be no need to draw, even. Harvard, with its robust budgets and famous faculty, was at the forefront of pushing a new Formalism and setting function and strength aside.

Reflecting on my cabin for Thoreau, I wondered whether it was the form or the function that had led me astray. I thought I had followed the directions and completed the assignment, but clearly something had been missing from my approach.

"Did you ask why we should build?" one instructor posed to me, when I asked for more feedback. "We cannot follow the assignments given to us. We have to ask why we should risk building anything at all."

———

For a next major assignment, we were asked to design a school of architecture. The site and form were up to us. But for the first time, we had to look at our surroundings and *ourselves* and question what architectural training is while we were being trained. It was a study in self-analysis. And looking at the world around us like through a hall of mirrors.

As the Yiddish maxim goes: "To a worm in horseradish, the whole world is horseradish." It was not so obvious to see how the Harvard GSD was shaping us until we could gain distance to see the ideas it had been built upon. And Cambridge was uniquely fit to provide this experience with its two major architecture schools, Harvard and MIT.

The Massachusetts Institute of Technology, now located on Cambridge's eastern end (though founded in Boston), set up the nation's first school of architecture in 1868. And Harvard, founded farther west in 1636 as the first university of any kind in the United States, opened its architecture school in 1874. But aside from agedness, the two have little in common.

Professor Wilson took our class on a field trip to MIT to interrogate the campus and understand what ideas drove its design.

MIT's architectural pedagogy (and many other academies across the world) was shaped by the École des Beaux-Arts, the premier French academy of fine arts and architecture. This school sought to lift architecture out of a model of in-field apprenticeship and into a formalized sphere of instruction where master architects developed their studio (or in the French, *atelier*) of students in a kind of lab.

The École des Beaux-Arts, the building, was not designed for architectural instruction per se, but instead was an adaptive reuse of an old convent. The old edifice was filled with desks and converted into a workshop space of production with generous room for other flexible use.

Wilson brought us to an MIT dormitory designed by the great Finnish architect Alvar Aalto, completed in 1949. The building sits along the Charles River, separated by Memorial Drive. The approach to the building is from the back, so the river is blocked, and we walked through a relatively congested street that felt like a service road. The redbrick building sits tall and thin, and it's shaped like an elongated horizontal "S." On the back side, large stair-shaped forms extend out from the façade and step up the building. The entrance is a single door leading into a glass foyer.

"I want you to run through and discover what you find," Wilson instructed as we filled the space. "Tell me the story of the building."

I began to take note of new details. The approach entrance splices through the center of the "S" shape, and the steps are gentle, creating a gradual approach into the glass foyer. Once inside, I encountered another half staircase beckoning me up to a landing filled with light and space that stretched beyond. A wooden handrail extended from the brick wall, drawing the hand. It was shaped in a unique way, with two curved humps, another "S" shape. "Hint number one," Wilson said, "the handrail is the plan." Aalto wanted you to physically feel the plan.

All around were the same set of materials. Bricks on the walls, slate dark tiles on the floors, and wooden trim for all the furniture and places where the body would touch the building.

I walked down the eastern hallway, which curved 90 degrees, and on my left encountered the stairs through an opening. They were generous and wide, and I immediately recognized that their form functioned as a way to traverse either side of the building's back façade. And each floor (there were six floors) had a landing along the route. In Aalto's design, he was building a complete world for the students who would move there. It was, after all, their new home.

At the sixth and top floor, a hallway extended beyond with dormitory rooms on the left-hand side and windows on the right. The dorm room windows faced the Charles River and the city of Boston beyond, with a window looking out from built-in desks with built-in closets behind. It was so humane. Every place the hand touched was wood. Every opportunity for view was taken, each room a careful ecosystem of student needs: space to sleep, space to study, space to store stuff. I was in awe of how one mind, one artist, could think of all these elements so comprehensively. The functional ambition, to allow every student a view of the river so they could learn with nature around them, was now clear as day.

I realized that the form and the function were working with each other here in balance, one not pushing the other, but both in concert. The beauty was tactile, in that at every moment when my body wanted to sit, or grab a handle, or touch a wall, it felt designed for that with soft wood and comfortable textiles where I might lay my hand. It felt like Aalto was guiding me through the building to stand, sit, look, walk, climb, and ponder.

Wilson reconvened us in the cafeteria space, which was shaped in a perfect square. "What did you discover?"

My classmates, now gathered around some of Aalto's plywood stools and chairs, responded:

"He leaves breadcrumbs of the concept through the building."

"No two levels are the same."

"I can't believe everyone gets to live surrounded by Aalto furniture," someone said. "It is such a warm and beautiful space."

"It is a puzzle he wants you to discover," said Wilson.

———

From Wilson's field trip, I saw the building as a lesson plan. He was teaching us to read like architects. He wanted us to see the pieces evident in our built world, everywhere, and make new and creative puzzles for us to live in and feel wonder within. To see the world that had been designed for us more clearly now.

Aalto's MIT structure was a course in architecture itself. Threshold, discovery, the puzzle of the plan, the search for logic and meaning, and the realization that the function, form, and beauty can all work in balance. There was no conflict. The dance Wilson took us to witness had made a lifelong impression of what to aim for, and what my first project had failed to achieve.

———

So how then does one design a school? Do we need classrooms to learn, or does learning happen amid the place, and among the entire campus? Or might we ask, why do we need spaces to help us learn at all?

The modern architectural movement that began after World War I, in which Aalto was a key character, had rethought tradition and legacy. The former educational models like the Beaux-Arts were tethered to a different era, and new industries and world political events demanded different educational experiences and different types of schools. The most ardent example was the Bauhaus, founded and led by Walter Gropius in Dessau, Germany, in 1919.

Gropius was a leading architect and designer who had led the new movement through teachings he had developed in Weimar, Germany. The Bauhaus had the aim of merging art, design, craftsmanship, and industrial processes together. Gropius's architectural school was unique in its approach to teaching, because instead of an atelier model of apprenticeship, women and men, artists and craftspeople alike would study color theory, film and photography, and furniture design all at once, in a more horizontal and comprehensive liberal pedagogical theory that sought to build a new religion of buildings, places, and people.

"Together let us desire, conceive, and create the new structure of the future," Gropius said in his Bauhaus Manifesto. "Architecture and sculpture and painting in one unity . . . which will one day rise toward heaven from the hands of a million workers like the crystal symbol of a new faith."

The Bauhaus school was itself an architectural thesis of how to merge industrial materials like aluminum and glass with hand-crafted elements of textiles and wood into unadorned, transparent, "honest" configurations. Housing for students and faculty was designed within the campus as clean straight lines, white walls, abundant light. It looked like a factory. Furniture designed at the Bauhaus was made from industrial materials and reconfigured natural ones, like molded, laminated plywood chairs and aluminum tubes more commonly used for bicycle handlebars. The Bauhaus approached all design work anew with a fever of designing a different world.

Gropius and others were influenced by the idea of *Gesamtkunstwerk*, a German word that means a "total work of art." In this, everything around, from the table to the dishware, to lighting, the windows, and the house itself should be "designed" with purpose and intent. Gesamtkunstwerk was an intentional, not inherited, approach to learning and practice. It asked us to read the world around us and ask why each thing we saw was designed that way, and could it be improved.

The Bauhaus principles took this idea literally, teaching everything from textiles, to furniture, ceramics, and weaving, to architecture itself. With the goal of transforming the way we work, live, and learn—and mixing the workshop with the atelier. They advocated that a redesigned environment could make us healthier and more connected to the world around us—as an effort to improve society by improving ourselves. And they taught these things in a space designed to these specifications and made to appear more like a factory without ornamentation and filigree. In such a space, we could see more clearly, without distraction and confusion, the purpose and potential of the things our hands had the privilege to build.

To understand how to design my own school, I naturally looked to Gropius's design of the Bauhaus campus. The plan of the Bauhaus separated out spaces for living, working, teaching, performing, and learning. One block was all studios for students (Prellerhaus studios), another all classrooms (the Technical College), and the two were connected by an administrative bridge that united the workshop block. In that section, amid workshop space, different rooms were called out in the plans for specific tasks like wall painting, veneer work, soldering, weaving, galvanizing, and others. On each floor a "master" would oversee each of these trades. This atelier hierarchy was still present here, but the Bauhaus spaces were purpose-built for tasks and trades that constrained the "freedom" of the masters to take learning off track.

The Bauhaus school was influential but short-lived. After only fourteen years, it was shut down by the Nazi regime in 1933, though at that point many of its faculty had scattered around the world, spreading its ethos to create a more "international style" of construction. And where they went they brought their version of teaching, learning, and practicing architecture with them. Gropius took an appointment at Harvard in 1937 and transformed it in the image of the Bauhaus. And from there elements of the practice spread throughout the American education system, which I found myself amid at Harvard now seventy years later.

Gropius's "Americanized" era brought some integrated ideas from the Bauhaus pedagogy but jettisoned others such as the specificity of workshops and trades. Harvard University had imposed its own storied culture and history back onto him. When Gund Hall was finally completed in 1972, a few years after Gropius's death, his ideas of the total school as workshop could be seen in the many disciplines and iconic open trays of the building.

Studying at Gund was learning from the long trail of influence of these early Beaux-Arts and Modernist teachers and how they envisioned spaces shaping how we learn.

Gund Hall was almost forty years old by the time I arrived. Its architect, John Andrews, sought a commonsense approach to design, where the spaces for learning—the trays—were also the social sphere. The instructional classrooms and administration offices would wrap the giant workshop space. Gund has it both ways. It takes the efficiency of the stacked tower (where offices and classrooms go) while spreading a tiered workshop across multiple levels—like a groundscraper covering many floors. It attempted to wrestle with the specificity of purpose-built spaces, while allowing a creative solution to the need for flexible, indeterminate zones.

It was quite an ingenious structure, and I began to see its influence from the École des Beaux-Arts, the Bauhaus, and other later postwar architectural schools. This research revealed that there was no one design for a school but rather that schools, as a rule, tend to be either purpose-built or free, rigid or open, and sometimes a mix of both. The plan of the school is a complex set of relationships of institutional boundaries, defined by authority of pedagogy, development of student culture, and the spatial relationships—classrooms, workshops, and hallways—of an open and evolving educational journey.

One faculty member at the Harvard Graduate School of Education summed it up more clearly. "We intend to shape students to go out into the world. The plan should be a diagram of the pedagogy we believe in. In the drawing itself, the arrangement of spaces and their use, one should be able to read the student the teachers seek to mold." I felt a little disoriented by this conclusion. Were the spaces I was learning in shaping me into a specific type of person? Was I becoming indoctrinated into a worldview, an ideology that I did not fully understand or buy into? And meanwhile I sat there, believing I had a choice in the matter, not understanding how much the space around me was shaping me into someone I did not fully comprehend.

To design a school then was to not mix a bunch of classrooms and teachers offices around a plan. To design a school was to design a culture. And to design a culture, one must ask a set of elemental and difficult questions about hierarchy, power, and sublimation. Such as those asked by an MIT architectural professor from the post–WWII era, Giancarlo De Carlo.

In his 1969 essay, "How/Why to Build School Buildings," De Carlo wrote:

> Authoritarianism and the aesthetics of order are correlated products of the rule of the class in power." He stated that, "No matter how different their appearances, the organizational structures of a school building can always be brought back to outlines based on the principle of authority: hierarchy of spaces, absence of osmosis between the different parts, interruption and control of internal and external communications, etc.

De Carlo proposed that any school—in order to resist its authoritarian impulses—should be more like a free series of spaces, working together amid an interconnected field of tranquil and open spaces. He called this an "unstable configuration" to create noninstitutional environments.

In designing schools, he and his contemporaries suggested an approach where the people and the collective students would participate in designing the spaces that they needed and in resisting at any cost the authoritarian impulses that the institutions inevitably perpetuate.

De Carlo was also an Italian activist who fought the fascists during

World War II. His approach to design and design education reflected his opposition to the overreach of authoritarianism of the 1940s. And when he designed his own architectural school in the 1970s, it would be a roving architectural study-abroad program, devoid of one building, and adaptable so as to bend with its various partners and hosts. He called it the International Laboratory of Architecture and Urban Design (ILAUD), and it attracted international students working together from 1976 to 2003.

But still, De Carlo admitted, no organization could fully lack hierarchy or power. Though they could be organized differently and spatially to resist it, the buildings themselves would reveal their organizational relationships and the culture they sought to foster.

De Carlo's provocations were hard to wrestle with in my mind. If all spaces produce some form of authoritarian control, how could it be ethical to design spaces at all? And as aspiring designers, how are we not ourselves being shaped and consumed by that taste of power itself?

———

Amid all the vocabulary, and philosophy, and technical instruction available to transfix the mind of a student new to architecture, there was one word perhaps as important as any that reminded us we were part of the lineage of the Beaux-Arts and the Western canon of architectural study: the *charrette,* or "little cart" in the original French. In the École des Beaux-Arts in Paris, instructors would wheel a cart around the open floor plan of the studio on the day of their final exhibition. The students, working furiously through the night and up to the last minute, drawing plans of their architectural designs, would then deposit their work on the little cart, the *charrette,* as it wheeled past their desk.

At architecture school, *charrette* becomes something more. It is both noun and verb. It is no longer a little cart, but a period before the final deadline of maddening, frenetic, and intense focus—when you finish your final projects, as students of architecture, you "go on charrette." But also, at the end of the semester of architecture school, everyone "charrettes" and finally decides what walls go where, and what roofs look like, and what concepts should hold together their architectural models and projects. Nothing like a deadline to push paralysis out of the corner and into action. The *charrette* is what makes and breaks the architect, indoctrinating them into a way of working that pushes their bodies and minds to the limit.

The final review of architecture school, that which we all "charrette" to, is a rite of passage. After an eye-blearing semester, the final two weeks become a mad mix of all-nighters and endurance tests to complete finished drawings, physical models, renderings, and a presentation. I did not know what I was getting into, but around me the studio space transformed from desks and floors to piles of paper, stained surfaces, toxic spray-booth fumes and burned chipboard, balsa wood clippings, and in general, an explosion of production. The student goes to an auditorium, stands up, and presents their project like in a theater, defending it and explaining it, and a jury of faculty and guests dismantle and poke holes in the assumptions and conclusions presented. The premise, the delivery, the performance all come under the auspices of critique, and it is not hard to feel as though, after a semester of work, all that was simply a preface to this public and personal attack.

When I stood up to finally show the project I had managed to compose, the jury patiently then impatiently took it apart, wall by wall, room by room. The approach to the site was clumsy, they told me, the form of the building had no voice, and the model and drawings and presentation created confusion of my intent instead of clarity. I knew the criticism was meant to be constructive and educative, but under so little sleep, with so much seemingly at stake, it was hard not to feel like it was personal, that I was being told, "You do not belong here." I felt like I had failed. I probably had.

For my first final review, I had been up for three days and so exhausted that I was not able to process the world around me while I was on *charrette*. I was so focused on completion the last few days that I had failed to check my cell phone once in the twenty-four hours before I presented. That turned out to be an issue on that final day, as I pulled out my phone post-bludgeoning to a barrage of missed calls and text messages—all from my mother and family.

"Where are you? Please pick up," one text read.

"We're in the ambulance, please call me," another said.

"Dad is going to the ER. He's gone into septic shock. Call me please!!" said a third.

I was standing in the vestibule of the GSD when I read these, near one of the hallways of only glass windows. I found a concrete wall to slide down into a seat on the brick floor. As I scrolled through the chain seeking resolution, paralysis and dread consumed my mind. What was the final text message, I wondered. Had he died while I was consumed with trying to prove I belonged in this world?

Just then a friend from home came into the building. My mother, not hearing from me, had contacted her to find me. "Your father is alive," she said and wrapped her arms around my limp body. "He was rushed to a hospital in New York City. He's in surgery but will be out in a few hours. I've come to get you and bring you there. To get you home."

———

We left, without my coat, without my model or drawings. Without knowing if I would come back. It was early December 2006, and it was bitter cold cold in the darkening Cambridge twilight.

Chapter 3

THE HOSPITAL

Butaro, Rwanda

Mom worked her whole life at or in hospitals. I couldn't stand the feeling I had in that space. And yet, my mother soldiered on every day of her career. I admired her for that. It was her workplace. And now, instead of being the nurse doing rounds, she was the family member holding the hands of a patient.

My father was admitted to Memorial Sloan Kettering, one of the great cancer institutions of the world, located in large towers that make up a half dozen city blocks around East 62nd Street in Manhattan. I met my mother there, and she escorted me through a set of doors, another hallway, and finally to Dad's room. It felt like entering a different world from Poughkeepsie.

———

The doctors were there, so I found a seat on the floor in the hallway as my sister, brother, mother, and I waited. The sounds of machines and loud voices and clanging doors ricocheted through the hall. In front of me was a framed print of Andrew Wyeth's painting

Christina's World, a peculiar choice for the environs. The gray sky and ochre grass were anything but hopeful.

On the walls underneath the print were railings, covered in a sort of plastic polymer that was yellowing and tan, that ran the length of the hallway. Down the hallway was a T-junction with another set of doors and another hallway cluttered with loose carts and unmanned equipment in both directions. From Dad's shared room, I'd learn, one could see the East River. But in this hallway—a "racetrack" in hospital parlance—there was just our family and the cacophony of blinking, beeping stuff.

Dad's doctor opened the door and introduced himself. He shook my hand and looked me in the eyes with the stare of a seasoned professional who was trained to give bad news, such as telling someone they were going to die. "We are rooting for you all," he said. "Your father is ready to see you."

I walked into his room first, and Dad looked at me with wide eyes. I could see he was afraid. He had been intubated and prepared for surgery. We were not sure he would wake up on the other end. Dad lifted his hand, raising his index finger, then pointing it at me. He was attempting to sign something. "What?" I laughed awkwardly. He did it again. One finger up, then pointing it at me. "I love you," he was trying to communicate.

"I love you too, Dad," I said. I put my hand over his toes and foot, over the blankets. I had never seen him so helpless.

Hours passed back in the waiting room, perched on hard plastic seats, *Judge Judy* on the television. It felt like the purgatory it had been designed to be. Then my mother called to say that Dad came out of surgery and survived. They had taken out a large coil of infected intestine and installed a colostomy bag.

We gathered again in Dad's hospital room, and only now did I have the wherewithal to notice how dull and cold it was. There was one chair for all of us, and it was covered in the many random bags we'd cobbled together, scurrying to make sense of the incomprehensible.

I found it confounding that a space like this was in one of the great institutions in the world. It felt so devoid of all the intent the care implied and that I knew architects had been taught to bring to our work.

I was shocked to see how few of the design lessons core to the profession had made their way into spaces of care. What made this place so indifferent to the human experience? Why the indignity? Where was the design?

The doctor sent us home with the same diagnosis we'd heard several years prior. Dad had, at best, a few months to live. It was like my mind split in half. He had beat it before, so why not now? I thought there must be a way he could survive. And I would believe that, despite the evidence or signs.

A few days later, I returned to Boston to finish my other finals at Harvard. I had tests and essays to complete the semester, and a father to honor while I still had him.

———

Most of us will spend time in a hospital during our lifetimes, yet architecture school had touched very little on these spaces during my first semester. The final days and nights back on campus were spent camped out in the trays. Mostly, we ate vending machine food from the fifth floor, but I did get out for the occasional meal in the square. Walking across campus on my way to dinner one of those nights, I noticed a flyer promoting a lecture by faculty member Paul Farmer, one of the most famous doctors in the world. I knew of Dr. Farmer from the book *Mountains Beyond Mountains*, which I had read while living in South Africa. In it, author Tracy Kidder chronicled Paul's work at first in Haiti and then around the globe fighting to provide health care to the world's least advantaged populations. He had started his organization, Partners In Health (PIH), while a student at Harvard and took root in Boston, having changed global medicine by focusing on the right to health care regardless of means or location. Coming to Harvard, I had hoped to meet him, and now I saw my chance. I asked if any of my architecture colleagues wanted to join me, but everyone was overwhelmed by end-of-year deadlines, so I snuck away to hear him speak in person.

I sat in the back of the small, packed room. I had arrived a little late and hoped to stay out of view. Paul spoke with chummy confidence, his speech laced with insider jokes and knowing looks at guests in the audience. Students, followers, and presumably staff were there to join the room full of Farmer fans.

He spoke about PIH's work on the global pandemic of HIV/AIDS, trying to get antiretroviral drugs to the communities in Haiti and elsewhere that could barely afford them. Haiti, he said, had seen incredible progress, but Haiti remained difficult. Generations of injustice, from America and beyond, were largely to blame. Dr. Farmer's tone lightened, however, when his topic moved to Rwanda, where PIH had opened an office just a year prior. The Rwandan president and minister of health were asking PIH to implement their philosophies of practice at a national scale with the government's full backing.

———

To my surprise, Dr. Farmer's words began with a focus on buildings rather than programs. He explained that PIH was constructing clinics in rural areas and had recently rebuilt an old hospital that had been abandoned during the Rwandan genocide. The existing hospitals were such a problem that PIH had taken to treating people inside their homes. Patients were suffering from "nosoco-mial infections" he said, hospital-borne infections that interacted with the immunocompromised populations within to create a truly deadly scenario.

Patients were walking into clinics with treatable physical injuries, like a broken bone, and leaving with maladies like drug-resistant tuberculosis, Farmer told us. And now, new diseases (or new super-powered strands of old diseases) were emerging from the facilities themselves. The hospitals had not been designed with these con-ditions in mind and were now functioning as vectors for disease. And while this was PIH's focus, their vision extended to improving treatment of noncommunicable diseases as well—ones like dia-betes and cancer.

My ears perked up. PIH was in a building phase: Hospitals, schools, roads, and infrastructure were needed to keep the com-munity healthy. Along with food programs, free health-care services, and bus transport for patients and their families, Paul said this work to remove the barriers to health might finally keep patients safe.

The people involved in PIH were clearly more than just doctors in low-income countries. These were systems planners, designers even, stitching together the fabric of a social sector that had long ago been disrupted.

Finally, he moved to the last leg of his plan. If a patient didn't have a place to live, he said, the drugs prescribed and care delivered would not take. The medicine was addressing what was in the body, but the root cause, the social determinants of what makes people get sick in the first place, he said that was what we must seek to cure.

He discussed the Program on Social and Economic Rights (POSER), a new effort that would, among other things, build houses for the people who were most in need of shelter.

―――――

I flashed back to my father and how our Poughkeepsie house had given him some elixir of purpose and potential, and I realized something. I had spent an entire semester crash-coursing on all the great buildings, architects, thinkers, styles and movements, patterns, rituals, and industry infighting in the world. But I had not heard anyone articulate the *why* of buildings as simply as Paul did in that lecture. He was saying that architecture could heal us. It could save a life. This changed everything for me. Architecture was no longer just academic; for Dr. Farmer, it was elemental, and it was urgent.

I waited in line for forty-five minutes after his remarks ended to introduce myself.

"I am an architecture student," I said. "I find your work so inspiring. Who are the architects working with you?"

"Architects?!" He laughed. "What architects? I drew the last hospital we built on a napkin." He looked at me, past me, and continued. "We build these ourselves. No architects have ever reached out to see how they can be helpful." I had hit a nerve.

"There is the school of architecture a block away. I'm sure anyone would get in line to work for you."

He looked at me with pity, like I had no idea how naïve I was.

"You could very well be the first architect to ask me, 'How can I help?' This is my colleague. She will give you my email. Shoot me a note and we can chat about it."

And then *poof*, he was gone.

Back at the studio late that night, I sent an email.

Paul, great to meet you. I was inspired by all that you said. I never thought of buildings this way. Is there any way I can work with you this summer?

He responded quickly:

It's not just buildings, the whole campus grounds and landscape are important to rethink. Find a way to get to us, and we can talk.

———

At the end of the first semester in architecture school, students scramble to set up their crucial first summer internships. Peppering firms in New York and Los Angeles with CVs and portfolios and statements of purpose in a race to get work experience, often at minimum wage, and sometimes for no pay at all. I saw a posting from a firm in San Francisco called Hart Howerton, offering a travel fellowship for students who applied with compelling proposals. I suggested a trip to Rwanda in support of PIH. A few weeks later I was accepted into Hart Howerton's first cohort, to spend half the summer in the San Francisco office and the other half helping Paul in Rwanda. I raced to my email to let Paul know the good news.

"I found the money to join you," I wrote.

"Everyone says they want to help," he sent back, "but 90% never find a way."

That spring semester was different from the fall. I started leaving school on Friday afternoons to drive back to Poughkeepsie to spend time with my father. I told him to hang on, and that I wanted him to see me get through the school year and come back from Rwanda.

———

He asked to come see me at school, making a trip with my mother to Boston to sit in on a midterm presentation. He walked in with an oxygen tank pulled behind him and sat wheezily in the back of the auditorium where I was presenting my project. My mother had a bag of medicine with her. "Parents do not usually come to these reviews," one of the faculty said, as if the awkwardness was my father's. "My husband wanted to see what exactly his son was learning," she said impatiently, and she glared at him for making her have to apologize for their intrusion.

Two weeks before my flight to commence my summer in San Francisco, my mother called to tell me through tears that Dad had died while away on a trip. He was with their closest friends, but it was going to take some effort to recover his body and prepare the funeral.

At that moment, I was mid-stride, walking into my studio instructor Laura Miller's office for my exit interview, and I remember this feeling of something being ripped out of me. I felt cavernous and empty—raw when I opened the door. Laura began to tear up telling me about her father passing the year before. I had walked into a new room I was not aware existed—a fellowship of dead fathers. It was a Friday morning in May, six months after the surgery. He had hung on as long as he could. And I would have to rush home to prepare a funeral before leaving for my summer job. The tasks piled into my lap. Design an invitation, organize the dropped-off macaroni dishes, pour wine, repeat. My brother and I would need to create the space for everyone else to mourn. Our time would come later—when it sunk in.

———

That June I left for Rwanda.

The first task on the day after arrival was to join Dr. Paul at a rural clinic to dig a fishpond. I, the aspiring architect, found myself halfway around the world with a team of doctors and public health experts, looking for meaning to be applied to the profession I had signed up for but so far didn't seem to belong in. They didn't seem to know what to do with me either. In those early days I would work on whichever odd jobs they could find, from finishing a waiting area outside the clinic to providing support on a new conference center. But on that first day, it was a fishpond.

The sun was hot and high, and the red dust of the dry season was settling on my clothes and in my nostrils.

"Come, sit next to me on this rock and tell me about your father," Paul said, feeling the weight I was carrying.

That was when Paul Farmer invited me in. Why were we here, together on a Saturday, digging a pond and laying bricks, and lifting stones as if our lives depended on it? And why, while we were doing that, was the first thought of this legendary, extremely busy man "Tell me about your grief"? How did he have the time, I thought, to sit me down and inquire about who I was? He gave me room to let it sink in. I felt my fatherly needs shift, filling the chasm and loss with this wonderful man whom I admired and whose affection I sought.

We were there to "beautify" the grounds of a medical center. We were laying stones, organizing bricks, and turning a mud field into a garden for the patients. Why did this justify equal importance to the medical work? I wondered. But Paul showed no such ambivalence. To be together side by side, laying bricks, planting trees, creating a home for fish to swim in, all in service to patients in need, this was the essential work.

Simple, easy solutions seemed inessential, until I heard Paul talk about them. "Dignificacíon," he called it. The process of how we would "construct dignity." Julio Frenk, then head of the Harvard School of Public Health, had said the same when he walked into PIH's hospital in Rwinkwavu. The construction of dignity, the beautification, this is what makes people feel as if they matter, even in the condition of limited resources. Design, the aesthetic realm, might inspire the brain, but it was providing a medical service for Frenk and Farmer, to show to people that "yes, even you matter to us."

———

Rwanda in 2007 was freshly tilled soil. Streets were swept, lawns were manicured, and education and health care were guaranteed. The genocide of 1994 had brought the country to depths to which humanity does not often fall. But thirteen years later, after focused investments in health, education, housing, economic reconstruction, and reconciliation, Rwanda had showed great signs that places could change. In 2008, at the height of the Great Recession, students from across Harvard—the medical, business, public health schools, and the college—made their way to Rwanda with open palms to add to the effort. It was a time of searching for stories of hope.

There was still a ton of work to do. After seeing what Partners In Health was capable of and what its focus on strengthening all the constituent parts of Rwanda's health systems would mean, the government was willing to invest even more deeply in its services.

That summer I was a rover between PIH sites, often crashing on random bunk beds in a shared dormitory. Every morning I rose early, diving into a project or shadowing dozens of experts as they went about their work. At the helm of much of it was the country director, Dr. Michael Rich, who was one of the leading doctors on the problems with multidrug-resistant tuberculosis internationally. But he was also connected with me through his status as an architectural buff and son of a contractor from the Boston area. And his head engineer, Bruce Nizeye, an expert builder from Rwanda, brought me to his workshops on the outskirts of the hospital campus in Rwinkwavu. There, three brick warehouses, remnants of a colonial Belgium mining operation, were filled with his teams. One was working on metalwork, another carpentry, and a third on equipment upgrades.

All the pieces of the buildings had been fabricated and constructed right there, on-site, with labor that Bruce had assembled. Bruce showed me how they made custom furniture, window frames, handrails, trusses, and even coffins for patients who passed away.

At school, we were taught to hire engineers, interior designers, and shop for furniture and windows from elaborate supplier catalogs. In the American context, custom pieces are often cost prohibitive. But here in Rwanda, custom was cheaper.

I was in awe. It was like the vision that Gropius had at the Bauhaus, *Gesamtkunstwerk*, a total work of design. Every piece of the hospital could be rethought from scratch—we just needed the designers, builders, and craftspeople to do so.

Michael Rich and I became close as we dove into the group's clinic plans. The hallways would need to be removed, he told me, because our patients were getting sicker in those places where they waited. In Rwinkwavu, the nation's poorest district, he had shepherded an old district clinic renovation into a vibrant national hospital. It was in rural and remote territory, bordering Tanzania and en route to the national game park, but it was buzzing. A brilliant composition of enthusiastic volunteers had arrived ready to chip in. There were the doctors visiting from PIH's outpost in Haiti, but also students of medicine, public health, and business from Harvard and a cohort of Rwanda's leading physicians, nurses, and medical researchers. Together, a vision of the future began to emerge.

We all gathered around Paul and his wife Didi's dining table in Kigali some nights and stood over plans and sketches, joined by doctors and government ministers, to think through how to execute the enormous project PIH had been called on to build: a comprehensive state health system. I'd leave that table with my mind cracked open to both the possibilities and urgency of putting my new discipline to real work for those who needed it most.

The government's next big investment was in the making, and they wanted to build a district hospital in the north, in a region called Butaro. It was hours from the capital, but there was an old army barracks that could potentially be earmarked for the site. Partners In Health would be the partnering organization. As a then-twenty-seven-year-old, I saw a building project imagined from its inception. It was exciting to see such a deal come together in person, among these brilliant dreamers over a belief. I remember the jolt of inspiration I felt. And then, right before I left, Michael took me aside.

"Could you help design it?"

When I returned to the US that fall, I didn't arrive with the same folder of summer work that my fellow graduate students had. They might have a set of visual renderings or sketches to add to a resume, or impressive works carried out at the behest of a well-established architectural practice. Instead, I had a finished laundry building, drawings of nascent housing developments, and an in-progress educational center that was under construction.

Partners In Health's leadership team asked me to present my work in their Boston office, under a title that would capture the question Paul had always seemed to be asking me:

"Can architecture save lives?"

After I spoke, Edward Nardell came over to speak with me. He was an infectious disease specialist at Harvard and worked at PIH on the study of tuberculosis. He had already immersed himself in the life I began to imagine as a pathway for my own while in Rwanda. Nardell pointed me to a study in Peru where older, colonial-era hospitals, built with generous windows, tall ceilings, and open-air waiting areas (before mechanical systems) prevented the transmission of tuberculosis better than newer buildings designed to keep mechanically conditioned air from leaking out.

Nardell told me that before air-conditioning, all hospitals were designed this way. They were based on the ideas of Florence Nightingale, whose 1859 *Notes on Hospitals* outlined the window sizes, room depths, and ceiling heights necessary to increase airflow and reduce disease transmission. It was kismet when, a month later, Paul Farmer's assistant Naomi sent me an email out of the blue. "We need to design that new hospital in Butaro, Rwanda," she wrote. "Paul told me to reach out and get you here."

———

After seeing my dad's suffering, I'd concluded that the hospital was a death sentence. You went there to die. But after a summer with PIH, I saw hospitals as more hopeful spaces of transition, where we, as patients, were meant to enter one way and leave another. Shadowing doctors, I'd also witnessed hospitals as workplaces full of the same frustrations and victories and joys, tiny and large, we all experience as professionals each day.

What resonated from all these experiences is how necessary it was for hospitals to function well. Their *utilitas* is so dominant that they represent the limited case of buildings whose usefulness renders their beauty and hospitality qualities almost tertiary.

Looking back at that time spent with my father, I remembered that his hospital provided care that few in the world could access: not only leading science but also restorative moments, like the view of the East River from his double room. Nonetheless, the hallways filled with beeping equipment, the waiting rooms dreary and windowless, the mazelike sequence from street to patient room, the sense of being lost in the institution will never leave me. My father's hospital had served both his humanity and his medical condition, but rarely both at the same time. I wanted those buildings to instead leave patients like him with a sense of wonder, and even hope, rather than the alienation and discomfort of being another warm body in a busy institution.

———

The Butaro Hospital would be PIH's largest single hospital project to date. When Paul invited me to join him and design this multimillion-dollar effort, with only a year of schooling under my belt, I was of course anxious about how I would pull something like this off. My marks in school had not been anything to write home about, and I could not imagine my lecturers would have seen me as the first choice for such a task. But all that considered, this was what had driven me to become an architect in the first place. If the experience with my father was true, that buildings could "save" or at least "extend" life—that they could heal injury and pain—what Paul had offered me was a chance to prove that with a hospital and a place that could have profound local and national impact. It felt as if there was no other choice but to dismiss the voices in my head (and the faculty in the school) telling me I was not ready. I had to take a leap.

I brought these thoughts with me as I prepared myself for the Butaro project. In researching, it became evident that hospital architecture provided an almost perfect illustration of the contradictions of architecture: the need to serve the population as well as the individual. To see this tension was to see buildings trying to shape our behavior. And in directing our behavior around critical services like health care, buildings could be considered to be advancing or suppressing our rights as members of a social body. Paul argued that health care was a human right, so a well-functioning hospital was not a luxury but the vessel to deliver and administer those rights. The alternative—a poorly designed hospital—was injurious and harmful. This was weighty stuff.

That January, I traveled back to Rwanda, to the site in Butaro, to see firsthand what stood before me. Michael Rich hosted me and two other design classmates of mine. Marika Shioiri-Clark, Alda Ly, and I began work as a cohort of designers working inside PIH and needed a name for ourselves. We landed on A Model of Architecture Serving Society (or MASS Design Group, for short) while sitting at Rich's eucalyptus wood dining table in Rwinkwavu. We kept designing the hospital through the spring back at Harvard, using empty GSD classrooms in the evenings with a few other students chipping in here and there while we assembled the project. We put our hearts into the work, passing up valuable time reserved for our studio projects to instead assemble something for Dr. Farmer and Dr. Rich that would prove they'd not been mistaken in entrusting us newbies with such an enormous task.

————

"It looks like a barracks."

The response was not what we were expecting.

"The problem is the hallways," Michael said when we presented our proposals. "The patients, they go in with one disease, they wait, and wait, and wait, they breathe on each other, and then they all leave infected."

Michael had studied this in rural clinics, where extensively drug-resistant tuberculosis (XDRTB) ran rampant and killed many previously uninfected patients who had contracted the disease while seeking care for other maladies. "We must do better," he said.

How do you build a clinic without hallways? We couldn't understand it, really. American hospitals had been nothing but hallways. Entrance to hallway, elevator to hallway, an endless labyrinth between building after building, never quite knowing where any path began or ended.

But Michael was insistent. Hospitals had figured this out once before. Consolidated pathways of travel, essentially superhighways for communicable disease, were to be avoided. First-world investment and obsession with technology had replaced timeworn lessons with massive mechanical air-handling systems that filtered infected air rather than avoid ingesting it to begin with. "That is designing for technology, not designing for disease," he told me, pointedly.

"In this condition, with limited resources, our best strategy is to move the patients outdoors," he said. "Move the waiting areas outdoors. Move the hallways outdoors. Keep patients in wards who need to stay inside and open the windows. If they are cold? Use a blanket. It is simple, age-old advice, and it works." Don't insist on customizing the world around you; instead, redesign the building with the world around you in mind.

"Do not worry," we were taught, "the engineer will handle it." Architecture school had always taught that the architect creates the form and then hires an engineer to handle the technical issues like air quality. That the design was one thing and the technology you insert into that design was another. But a hospital requires a lot more of that engineered stuff that I did not fully understand. Invisible airborne pathogens, expelled in the millions by a simple cough, were the source of a rampant TB epidemic that had taken root in Rwanda. And without a design response, these illnesses would prevail. It hit me, the buildings around us could be a solution to these deadly diseases. The outside, where air flowed freely and pathogens were far less likely to transmit from person to person, needed to be brought inside.

———

Buildings, the architecture around us, are quite like giant air filters. The window, that beautiful feature of the façade, is actually a pretty sophisticated technology. It brings air in and allows air to flow out. It provides light and can be shaded to provide privacy at night. And in the context of the hospital, it could be opened by patients to mix in fresh air with vulnerable air indoors, but then closed if needed to retain heat in the cold.

We were all moving toward something like an open-air ward, but I couldn't help wonder if this was less of a fix than it was a makeshift solution for the poor, used because mechanical systems were too costly, expert care too difficult to access, and the patients too disempowered to push back. But Dr. Rich was adamant we'd landed on a superior, not spendthrift, solution that would work in Rwanda and anywhere in the world. The design of the institutional hospital had created this problem, and we needed to redesign it root to stem to solve for the evolving nature of health. "What we are doing here is even more modern than the hospitals we trained at in Boston," he said. In those facilities, he reminded me, the windows were sealed shut for all.

Here, looking backward was the way forward. What I did not know then was these such experiments in the field were preparing me for something closer to home a decade later, during the outbreak of the COVID pandemic.

More immediately, the real world had come calling. Faced with the decision to choose training or practice, I decided to take a break from Harvard. Paul and Michael Rich had entrusted me to support them in the design of their new facilities, but had no money to support me. I took alternative measures and applied for grants to get myself and a few others out to Rwanda semi-permanently to support the design and construction over the next year.

Days were consumed with drawing up plans and nights focused on explanations of progress to the doctors. Skepticism abounded. Until proposals became reality, the team of unproven designers would remain a more risky flight of fancy than a stroke of brilliant talent identification by Michael and Paul. We felt the pressure to demonstrate that our design, the investments attached, and the work we'd done were worthy of PIH's confidence.

———

When Florence Nightingale spread word to see hospitals as living systems that needed to be calibrated to move air through them, the enemy was "miasmatic air." Before the germ theory of disease was pioneered by Louis Pasteur and Robert Koch in the late 1800s, it was widely believed that unpleasant smells—miasmas—were themselves the cause of any number of diseases.

The urban street in the 1850s was not only filled with people and transportation but piles of waste, rotting carcasses, trash, open sewers, smoke, and industrial pollution. The smells were to most minds the direct cause of the maladies that ran wild in cities like Manchester, London, New York, and Boston.

Nightingale, however, had been a nurse during the Crimean War, where British troops were stationed in what is now modern Turkey, in the coastal town of Renkioi. Many patients in the medical clinic were dying, not from their battle wounds but from the time spent in the clinic that was meant to treat them. An engineer from London (Isambard Kingdom Brunel) proposed a different clinic design to address the problem—raised off the muddy ground, with plentiful windows and a hand crank to push fresh air constantly through the facility. Patients sitting on raised beds instead of the ground recovered at an astonishing rate, with improvements of up to 40 percent reduction in deaths. Nightingale had grown accustomed as a nurse to seeing injury and disease as death sentences, but now was watching patients recover and return to the battlefield.

Armed with this insight, Nightingale authored *Notes on Hospitals*, which established rules for how all health-care facilities should be built. She wasn't designing a specific building, but rather creating a code, or set of rules, for how hospitals should be constructed, with health outcomes as the primary focus. Health, above all else, was the criterion by which hospitals should be judged, and achieving those outcomes required a well-designed space. Without this, she argued, such outcomes would be impossible.

Nightingale's strategies were simple: Wards needed to be filled with natural light and have generous windows. They also needed to be small enough to avoid overcrowding, with a maximum of thirty-six beds per ward and not too many doctors rotating through. Early hospitals of the eighteenth century, like the Hôtel-Dieu in Paris, housed up to two thousand patients in large, open rooms—sometimes two or three to a bed—resulting in diseases spreading rapidly and high mortality rates. By breaking the ward into smaller sections, outbreaks could be contained more effectively when they occurred.

In Rwanda, as in many other rural clinics, these basic parameters were difficult to find. The World Bank had been paying for clinics and using the same design over the entire country—a rectangle, with a hallway down the center, and rooms on either side. Put a gabled roof on it for the entire length and call it a functional clinic building. "The problem is," Michael Rich told me, "that this basic design is terrible." This model put patients together, out in an enclosed hallway without ventilation.

To tackle overcrowding and attack the hallway problem, we slightly modified the Nightingale ward concept. The central pathway was replaced by a half-height wall. Beds were then extended outward from this wall, with the headboards of those beds facing patients out toward the windows and away from each other.

This helped, but the solution was something even more elemental. If hospital hallways were making people sicker, let's design one that doesn't need them at all. Instead, the structure could be designed where all patients, staff, and public movement took place outdoors. The temperate climate of Rwanda allowed for comfortable outdoor waiting areas most of the year, and covered spaces would offer shelter during the rain.

This design required a multibuilding layout rather than a single sprawling institution. Each building would be narrow enough to allow air to circulate freely, with windows on both sides of the structure to enhance ventilation. Doctors would navigate between buildings on foot, through a landscape of lush gardens, with covered pathways directing their journeys.

Our facility would also need to be fully accessible without the use of elevators, a technology prone to breakdown and high maintenance costs. Inspired by the zigzagging footpaths of Rwanda's hills, we layered the hospital across one of them, ensuring that multiple stories would remain accessible at ground level, while also leaving room for future expansion.

And finally, we needed to address the heartbeat of the hospital. How could we facilitate better working conditions and patient access for the nurses who provided direct care each day? I offered the idea of situating nurses' stations at the centers of open wards. The station would consist of low, immovable walls that provided visibility across the entire facility. These would be built to avoid any obstructions that could block sight lines between staff and patients. At the end of each ward, we'd include glass-doored isolation rooms for actively contagious patients, with adjacent bathrooms designed to minimize the spread of odors and bioaerosols through dedicated venting and entrances. In doing so, the nursing staff would be able to monitor multiple patients at once without endangering themselves or the other individuals seeking care at the same time.

This revised idea of the clinic also revealed the deeper role for architecture. By orienting beds toward the windows, patients could enjoy breathtaking views of the landscape outside. Research has shown that access to an outside view reduces hospital stays and lowers pain medication requests. And with beds no longer lining the ward's periphery, we could enlarge the windows, lowering their sills below headboard height to flood the space with light and fresh air. This design demonstrated that the utilitarian needs of architecture can still center on human needs by harmonizing function, form, and experience.

———

The iconic hills of Rwanda sit atop volcanic rock, and homes and gardens are often built from basalt—igneous rock shaped by the earth's fiery past. Butaro sits at the edge of the Virunga Mountain chain, rich with this black, porous stone that is not just abundant but ideal for construction. Its malleable texture makes it easy to shape, and the locals have long used it in their buildings, layering stones thick with mortar or sometimes smoothing them over with hand-applied cement, creating a textured patchwork that speaks to both necessity and craft.

But I wanted something different for the hospital. Something more precise, more intentional—an echo of the dry-stacked garden walls that seamlessly fit together, as if the stones themselves knew their place. The idea was simple, but making it a reality required ingenuity and skill. Nizeye, the lead builder, was adamant: We needed mock-ups first. He hired the best masons he could find, and together they began experimenting. We found ourselves out in the pitch-black night, illuminating the samples with car headlights, searching for the right combination. Some mock-ups used too much mortar; others lacked the variation I wanted. But one—the last one—stood out: a perfect assembly of stone, each piece unique, with joints so tight the mortar was barely visible. That was it.

At dawn, the masons got to work. Anne Marie Nyiranshimi-yimana, a mason who had founded a guild of female workers, traveled two hours to lend her expertise. Alongside her was Emmanuel Hakizama, who was still training but eager to learn. Together with their colleagues, they began cladding the walls of the hospital's largest and most visible building—the first that patients would see, and the one that needed to set the tone. The stones were stacked carefully, each one finding its place, and as the weeks passed, the masons developed new techniques that made use of the resources at hand. We repurposed clothes hangers to measure and then match stones to one another with precision. Before long the massive thirty-foot central wall of the structure took shape.

When the team finally reached the corner where they had begun, the improvement in their craftsmanship was undeniable. They asked if they could add to the original work and rebuild it to meet their new standards. It would cause a delay, but Nizeye agreed, recognizing that the quality of the final product was worth the wait.

Piece by piece, the hospital was brought to life by the hands of local artisans. And not just the walls, but the furniture and windows, too, were were handmade from Bruce's workshops. In the end, it became more than a building—it was a symbol of purpose, intention, and community. This was not about the abstract ideals of architecture that had dominated my education. This was something different: the creation of beauty from the simplest materials, by the hands of those who knew them best. Stone and hand, brought together in the most fundamental act of building. This was beauty, pure and essential.

The stone walls were also a symbol of regional economic impact. These were constructed of cheap, sometimes discarded materials. But now, the clinic showed the stone in a different light, with a value that could be reevaluated and redeployed. After completing the hospital, some masons were asked to build in other places in the country utilizing similar designs and techniques, including in the capital, Kigali, for a homeowner who saw pictures of the hospital and wanted that same wall in his home.

The telltale volcanic rock was a national symbol of pride and potential. Other projects followed, and a guild-like system of expert masons emerged, forged by the stone walls of Butaro Hospital. The hospital had become not only a needed public health investment but also a regional job creator and economic development project.

When we had to excavate the hill, hundreds of laborers gathered to work on the site, making good wages that would more typically be given to contractors imported from the south of the country. Partners In Health knew that jobs, wages, and housing were essential elements to the social determinants of health, so providing jobs was just another element of the immense potential of this project. And we set off to do just that. It all brought to mind a lesson Bruce taught me about a local word in Rwanda called *ubudehe*, which translates roughly to "community works, for the community."

The architect, I came to realize there, wielded hidden power. She was not merely the holder of the drawing, she specified materials and with those materials who could be employed, and so design decisions needed to be made to positively impact the place where building is done. Those decisions needed to consider the "who" for the builds as well as the "how" the building project will be built, not just the "what" we build. I learned all these lessons just working with my hands on that hill for Bruce and Michael and Paul. It was my field's responsibility to push for change where we could achieve it.

"With limited resources," Farmer once said to me, "people get resourceful." This was certainly what I'd observed in Butaro. The new ward design was a hit. The government asked us to write its parameters into new national policy. Every trip to the site seemed to encounter something new. I began to see all along the road new businesses opening and new investment in infrastructure like roads and fiber optics being laid. A Bilbao effect, but in Rwanda.

Nonetheless, I was cornered by a skeptical field surgeon at a PIH fundraiser event where the hospital was featured. "I thought what you were doing was an enormous waste of time and resources," he admitted. "We doctors look for proof and evidence; it is hard to quantify the value of design. But when I saw the stone walls, I realized we needed this, too. The unquantifiable, and the beautiful, is also in the service of our patients and their health."

He was right. The work in Rwanda was risky. And at times, I did not know how we were going to complete the hospital. But with it nearing completion, all sorts of new possibilities emerged, and concepts I had begun to imagine in school became facts to me, proven on the hills of Butaro.

On that hilltop in Rwanda, Nizeye, the stonemasons, and the doctor taught me something I had not learned in architecture school. They taught me that architecture can both impede and advance our collective rights—such as the right to health care or the right to breathe. But they also taught me that buildings, when made with great care, can help us locate ourselves within the sometimes dizzying and alienating pressures of the world around us. They locate us and ground us, and through this they give us hope. Buildings can fulfill our most elemental right—the right to dignity.

———

After over a year on the ground and with designs complete, I was finally able to move back to Cambridge and manage from afar. But I needed people on the ground in Butaro to help oversee. With the small budget left in my travel grants, I was connected through friends to some talented people who, as it turned out, were also searching for something different in their careers. Hart Howerton continued to support me, and Cody Birkey, an employee whom I had befriended in San Francisco, got clearance to move to Rwanda to help with the construction project for the year. Another architect and a former Peace Corps member, Garret Gantner, reached out and applied to work on the Rwanda project as well. And other connections from the office and back home began to assemble as volunteers to help keep the momentum going. A friend of a friend, Sierra Bainbridge, moved to Rwanda to take my spot leading the office, coming in shortly after helping design the High Line in New York City.

This project I started had become bigger than itself, and armed with this experience and the help of classmates on what a design firm of my own could look like, the formal founding of MASS Design Group—from a circle of friends interested in changing design to a firm actually putting those interests into action—came together. We set out with a nonprofit model inspired by how PIH worked alongside its patients to uncover the designs that would amplify the lives of those interfacing with them. We wanted partners, not just clients.

Despite all the excitement around MASS Design, I was still scraping by as a student as I neared completion of architecture school. I had over $250,000 in student loans hanging over my head, racked up between undergraduate studies and my graduate degree that had been extended out over the early work of building a practice. It was my loans, travel grants, and credit card that had been our seed capital. Regardless, things were humming in Rwanda, with nearly five full-time people from both Rwanda and the US, and MASS had begun to add people to support from Boston. Other classmates even decided to join full-time postgraduation, like Alan Ricks and David Saladik, who had been involved in early *charrettes* around the GSD. These were all signs that there was a realness beginning to take shape of this alternative path toward building a practice. In those early days, we could barely pay ourselves anything, relying on what remained of early grants we could cobble together, my credit card, and the few fee-paying (often subsidized to support fledgling nonprofits like MASS) domestic projects that began to trickle in. Things were unsettled but approaching something stable, sure, and resilient to the machinations of the world around us.

But then, I found myself opening a new email from Dr. Paul's office. This one titled simply "Tragedy":

An earthquake in Haiti has struck. I wanted to let you know. The devastation is overwhelming. Buildings collapsed, death everywhere. Many of our doctors and their families were affected. I will keep you abreast. We could use some architects as we imagine rebuilding.

It was January 12, 2010. Little did I know how much this event would set in motion.

Chapter 4

THE LATRINE

Port-au-Prince, Haiti

Port-au-Prince International Airport in the wake of the 2010 earthquake was, in a word, chaotic. Dr. Patrick, a Haitian doctor I'd met in Rwanda, sent an invitation to observe the damage and assess how our team could help.

Traffic in Port-au-Prince, through the rubble and crowds of people, alongside military personnel in tactical gear wielding long rifles, was almost unimaginable. A two-lane road was being used as a six-lane highway, with cars taking over sidewalks and four lanes heading in one direction and two in the opposite. Then we drove along Route de Delmas 18, descending from the hilly outskirts of Port-au-Prince, which sits in a bowl-like formation surrounded by distant mountains. Multistory concrete buildings lay flattened like pancakes, their columns crumbled beneath collapsed floors, now just piles of horizontal slabs surrounded by debris. Each wreckage a testament to structural failure.

We drove to the Saint Gérard neighborhood, renowned for its charming gingerbread houses. This area, once the enclave of the Haitian elite, was now transformed into a mix of architectural styles.

Gorgeous wooden houses with a distinctive aesthetic lined the streets, featuring grand verandas, soaring ceilings, intricate floor tiles, and ornate hand-carved details. The lush surroundings included palm trees and vibrant potted plants. While some buildings showed signs of partial collapse, many more had remained intact, unlike elsewhere on the island.

We arrived at the Hotel Oloffson, famed as a place where artists, musicians, and travelers had gathered for years, and where Graham Greene wrote his book *The Comedians* about Haiti. Remarkably, the hotel showed no signs of damage.

Upon investigation and meeting with the locals, the Oloffson had benefited from being "out of date." Its wooden bones did a better job at absorbing the shock of the quake than more modern concrete construction that essentially crumbled under the stress.

Patrick then took me to the Haitian national palace, the president's official residence, where its signature domes had collapsed. After that we headed to the main park downtown, where a tent city had quickly popped up to house the nearly twenty thousand people who had been immediately rendered homeless in the catastrophe. The victims stationed there formed an instant community, wrapped in USAID blankets that read, "From the American People."

It was clear the situation was critical and nowhere near sufficient for the needs of the moment. The international groups had their procurement systems in place, but the housing situation was not up to the moment. Port-au-Prince didn't just need a new tent design; it needed a redesign of how it was preparing itself for the disasters to come as well. It needed a medium-term structural solution that, ideally, could serve as a model for the future of this place.

Eric Cesal, who was leading the Architecture for Humanity (AFH) response on the ground, agreed. His group had feared Haiti was walking to the edge of disaster even before the earthquake struck.

AFH was already involved in plans to build schools and housing outside the Port-au-Prince city center, a move that would, in theory, make things more habitable and put people less at risk and easier to care for in the event an emergent condition came around. But now as dollars came in and needs continued to grow, efficiency and speed began to win the argument.

The country was rich with inspiring old architecture and had now seen evidence that rushed, utilitarian building had left it vulnerable to an extraordinary extent. Were we really going to repeat the same mistakes?

———

Eric and AFH had valuable insight to take advantage of in this unsettled post-earthquake period. They had been on the ground for a year now and seen the hardship of construction in the face of the institutional and financial constraints present. Several of Eric's team's projects had gotten off the ground enthusiastically before languishing with inadequate support or—even worse—not treated seriously by those who'd previously committed to follow through on their claimed hope for Haiti's future.

"Everyone wants to send us shipping containers for houses," Eric told me, rolling his eyes. Instructions to build a new Haiti from recycled and substandard parts came from far and wide. I remembered Paul Farmer warning me about this once, back when we were together planning for Rwanda. The "first world's" seeming ignorance of what it meant that solutions for places like these were often literally to send our garbage and expect a hero's treatment in return.

Other international efforts focused their attentions elsewhere as pitches came in for all sorts of prefabricated housing solutions—things like flat-packed houses that could be shipped to Haiti and erected immediately. I maintained my appreciation for the advantages of more traditional Haitian construction, but speed and immediate recovery were clearly important in this emergency context.

In the United States, a prefabrication movement had already taken hold—where buildings, rooms, or houses were being built and manufactured in factories off-site before being assembled at their intended destinations. The US had its own housing crisis to address—one that has only gotten worse since then—and needed ways to accelerate the creation of new housing stock for its ever-growing population. Prefabs offered simple, industrially identical, rapidly deployed builds. They were especially well fit for the US because that last step—the on-site building process—was where costs typically began to balloon. Prefabrication meant that last-minute labor crises were kept to a minimum, and the costs of the materials required for the build became a wholly known factor up front.

Notably, the cracks that led to catastrophic collapses were often due to corners being cut in situ. Rebar wasn't tied correctly, or engineering drawings, presumably stamped by the local architectural commission, weren't followed. Prefabrication could help with this, sure, but in poor economies, that extra labor or material could be the difference between eating or not that night. So corners get cut, and when they do, it creates an Achilles' heel for the project. Hidden away and covered over in stucco or cement, the fault lines don't show until the ground shakes.

But in Rwanda, I learned the lesson was more complex. Labor was very inexpensive, and materials were cheap. The equation was backward. The stone wall we built in Butaro had been about *maximizing* labor costs, not minimizing them. We knew that every dollar spent there was being reinvested into the pockets of local residents and making them part of the project itself.

In Haiti, this also made sense. People needed jobs, and the money being spent by the aid economy now taking over the country should benefit as many locals as possible. Speed was an issue, but fidelity to strength was just as urgent. The extreme circumstances of the time meant we couldn't wait years to erect these houses, but we also could not afford to erect houses that would not stand the test of time. And so, something in-between (something locally fabricated with prefabricated materials) prevailed, which would allow minimal finishing on-site without sacrificing labor. I wrote down in my notebook *Local-fabrication,* or LOFAB, as an answer to how we could transform our work to something greater—a catalyst of economic reconstruction and investment.

———

In Rwanda, I had begun to think of buildings as something different—containers of air, complex filters, controlling what enters and exits, determining what we breathe, differentiating the inside and the outside. Architecture was no longer just about space, but about life itself.

But Haiti shattered and rebuilt this understanding again. When I arrived after the earthquake, a horrifying realization emerged: People had not just died because of a natural disaster—they died because of the failure of the buildings around them. Over 250,000 souls were lost not just to shifting earth but to collapsed concrete, to structures that could not withstand a crisis they should have been designed for.

"Architecture did this" was my initial, disturbing thought. But it wasn't just that. The deeper and broader system that demands buildings to be built with compromises in place was to blame as well. Over time and with changing priorities, the business of building had abandoned its most elemental requirements. It was a sobering truth: The structures that should protect us had become instruments of destruction. Their failure of *firmitas,* the essential principle of strength, exposed a deeper failure of society to fully account for the dignity and safety of human life.

The global financial collapse of 2008 had left architecture at its nadir. Firms shuttered, cultural projects stalled, and architects—once creators of monuments and cultural beacons—were left wondering if their work mattered at all. Haiti reframed that question, demanding not only that we design, but that we roll up our sleeves and learn to serve a different clientele, because designing for survival drilled down to the marrow of what we'd studied to practice all along.

Aid groups like USAID and the UN were rapid in their response, setting up emergency shelters, tent cities, and temporary housing solutions. But this wasn't enough. You can erect tents and give shelter to people in need, but what about the water they drink, the waste they generate, the invisible threats of disease lurking in the untreated sewage flowing through the streets? What about the clinics that would be built without thought of the hallways where patients would get sick?

There was more work I could do here.

Aid organizations like Médecins Sans Frontières and USAID had long ago perfected the logistics of emergency shelter. Yet, many of us in architecture were still consumed with the design of the tent itself, missing the larger issue: How do we move from temporary shelter to *permanent*, resilient homes?

Haiti quickly became a crucible for a shift in the profession. The rush of attention on the humanitarian crisis in Port-au-Prince, a place where necessity and design collided, meant that architecture could no longer afford to sit on the sidelines, waiting for the next cultural commission. We were reminded that beneath the attention-grabbing exteriors sat crucial systems—water, sanitation, education—that address the structural forces keeping people in poverty. Architecture was essential, a tool for survival, a vehicle for justice and repair.

In medicine, the proximal is the wound you treat immediately; the distal is the root cause, the social conditions that led to the injury in the first place. Architecture had to do both. It had to stop the bleeding while addressing the deeper, systemic issues at play.

Haiti was a link in a broader failure of our built environment where safe, affordable, and decent housing failed to meet the needs of an urbanizing planet. In refugee settlements across the world, the aid industry had grown complacent putting distressed people into "emergency" shelter for sometimes twenty years. The temporary had become semipermanent, and when media attention waned after the initial crisis incident, those left behind would now be stuck with something insufficient for a well-lived life, development, or growth beyond the most threadbare existence.

First, there are the immediate needs of shelter—urgent, flat-packed, shipped in, and deployed. The design solutions are not about form but about deployment, about transport efficiencies, volume, and speed to responsiveness. The design is in the delivery.

Second, there is the long-term, permanent work we were taught to focus on in school. Monuments, cultural projects, the president's palace, the national theater, the iron market in Haiti, the monument to liberation, and the parliament building, or even the famous hotels like the Oloffson. These are symbols, landmarks, important cultural artifacts whose design is generational. They should outlast us and protect us into the future. Our children should experience them as we have, see what we see, and so too their children. We are taught to engineer these buildings for one hundred years, and we imagine them in generational time.

But third, in between the emergency shelter and the generational time of the cultural assets, is everything else. The vast majority of all buildings lie in the middle and last only twenty to thirty years before they are deconstructed or replaced. This is customary. So if temporary structures were being kept in place for as long as buildings built for a century, why not change our practices to build for the *middle term* and meet the immediate need in ways that recognize the reality of how these structures will likely be used in practice? When it came to clinics and hospitals, people understood that this balance could be struck. But what was still lacking is the recognition that the whole lives of those in need could be undermined by not making the same demands for their conventional living spaces as well.

———

As if the earthquake wasn't enough, cholera arrived next. The outbreak spread rapidly through Haiti's broken water systems, winding its way through and into places that had perceived themselves as apart from the devastation. The GHESKIO clinic stood on Boulevard Harry Truman, its walls surrounding an orderly, well-maintained campus fit with manicured grounds and sprawling buildings, whitewashed and interconnected. But inside there was chaos.

We'd been called here and gathered in a conference room with tiled floors and a long table. Soon the room filled with doctors in white coats, one of which was an august older man who introduced himself with a warm "Call me Bill." This was Dr. Jean "Bill" Pape, a legendary figure in Haiti's medical community.

Dr. Pape told us we were on the grounds of the world's first AIDS clinic he had established in 1982, where he'd worked before his most recent appointment to the faculty of the Weill Cornell Medical College. He was a leader in global infectious disease research. He had steadily grown the clinic into the largest health-care provider in the capital city, all while navigating the country's whiplashing political turbulence.

"I don't like to get too involved in politics," he told me quietly, but the subtext was clear. A lack of cooperation would disrupt his urgent and necessary work.

He explained that in the first ten weeks of the cholera epidemic in October 2010, every province had cases to report. In the first five months, over 4,500 people had died, leading to the worst global cholera epidemic in a century. By the end, nearly 800,000 people would be infected. The aid focus had shifted from permanent housing to emergency tents, but some funding had become available to build a new, semipermanent structure specifically to rehydrate and rehabilitate those impacted. He needed architectural help immediately to secure the grant and begin construction. As he detailed the needs demanded by cholera and other diarrheal diseases, we walked outside to the busy boulevard.

"That's our patient population right now," he said, pointing across the street. There, in the midst of a different city, waste piled on the streets, frogmen manually emptied cesspools when they overflowed. The message was clear from the somber tone of his voice. "These people—if we don't help them—they will die."

I moved through the crowded street, dodging tap-tap taxis and weaving between heaps of refuse. Water and waste pooled in the corners, infecting more people each day. The sights were, in a word, distressing. But at the same time there was a ray of hope lent by familiarity—this beast Cholera, I knew now, had a means and method to address it.

For the past three years in Rwanda, in the quiet of night and at daybreak, I read. I'd taken to reading as much about epidemics as I had about architecture. And this new challenge had struck a chord.

———

Cholera has a way of revealing both what it needs and what it takes. Water, that necessary nourishment, when contaminated, is also the poison that empties the body of its fluids. Patients who get cholera must endure a devastating dehydration once called "the wasting death," where they become so emaciated that their systems fail.

London's system was once failing, too. In the 1850s, it was a rapidly growing city, but beneath its streets lay an invisible threat: the stench and squalor of untreated human waste.

In pre-1850s England, before the advent of modern indoor plumbing and sewer systems, the "bathroom" was in most cases an outhouse or privy, a small shack usually located outdoors that housed a basic toilet, often just a seat over a pit. These cesspits would eventually fill up, leading to contamination of the ground or nearby water sources. Wealthier households had more elaborate arrangements, but even they relied on chamber pots, servants to clean them, and soil men—workers who would come to empty the contents of these containers, often during the night, and dump their contents into the streets, open cesspools, or the river Thames itself, which made sanitation the urgent crisis of the industrial era.

The lack of proper sanitation infrastructure meant that waste disposal was left to be a personal or localized problem, ruling out the mass public development needed to address the spread of disease in the cramped, unsanitary conditions of rapidly growing cities. The few public toilets that existed were generally unhygienic, often nothing more than holes in the ground or shared outhouses in alleys.

The lack of a modern sewer system meant that human waste disposal was primitive, and as the population soared, so did the scale of this public health disaster. It was common that waste, allowed to mix with sources of drinking water, would spread disease. But medical professionals did not confirm that suspicion until 1854.

The term *miasma* still carried the day. As people piled waste out of sight or the range of their noses and into open drains or dumped directly into the Thames River, the city silently became a breeding ground for waterborne diseases.

It was in this grim setting that John Snow, a local physician, made his revolutionary discovery: Cholera wasn't spread by the air, but through the water. His investigation of the Broad Street pump in Soho traced a cholera outbreak to a single water source. He saw the water pump's pipe broken, mixing with open sewage, and realized this contamination was waterborne, not "miasma, air, or morally"–borne.

This discovery would change cities forever. It would usher in the modern sanitation movement and, in its wake, the discipline of urban design as an outgrowth of epidemiology. London shifted its priorities to focus on sanitation and public health. In 1859, construction began on a new sewer system designed by Joseph Bazalgette, eventually finished in 1875. This system, a marvel of Victorian engineering, would eventually bring clean water and proper sewage treatment to the city, helping end the cycle of cholera outbreak and shepherding in the modern metropolis.

Cities the world over copied this essential and necessary public works project to solve their similar health nightmares. Streets were dug up, sewers laid beneath, and now the city itself was interconnected through a vast and largely invisible labyrinth of sewer pipes and distribution pools.

With modern sewers, however, these public privies became more private, as they could now be linked into the broader public sewer itself. The modern city sewer system ushered in the modern bathroom, and consequently (and perhaps not so evident from day-to-day experience) all buildings began to be designed around their city's plumbing systems. This monumental shift essentially created the principle of "privacy" as we know it, while also keeping populations in place and healthier.

At the same time this change would also shepherd in a less direct relationship to the waste we emit onto the world, and its consequences, when we no longer saw and smelled it ourselves each day.

———

I heard doctors refer to bathrooms as where humans "exit." I thought that fitting. The toilet, the privy, the water closet, the commode— what we now call the bathroom—is where the body exits its waste; but it is also a type of portal, to what links the architectures of our world to each other. It is for most our clearest tie to the public infrastructure that surrounds us at all times. It forces what was once visible (and smellable) to become invisible, literally under the ground, out of sight and out of mind. The sewer pipes that led to bathrooms had become like the built world's equivalent to the roots of plants, defined by a linked, interconnected grid beneath our neighborhoods, like some broad and invisible rhizomatic entity, emerging into our worlds to define the grids of our neighborhoods.

On a driving tour through rural KwaZulu-Natal in South Africa in 2009, I saw this in practice. A new housing development was under construction along the side of the road. It had a hundred houses or so, public, for the poor, built by the state. But the houses were not built yet. All that was built was a field of bathrooms, on a perfect grid, with the recent dirt between them linking them together. The bathroom, a prefabricated unit, came plugged in, and the house would eventually be built around it. In terms of functionality and strength, the toilet is the cornerstone of our health. It is also the least flexible part of any dwelling. The most private, but the least mutable.

———

In college, I had studied Elaine Scarry's *The Body in Pain*, a book about how the mind endures when the body breaks down when subjugated and tortured. One of the key concepts is that in the bathroom, we are both comforted by and haunted by what our body is capable of, and the bathroom keeps that abjection at bay. Those words stuck with me as I became responsible for managing those fraught relationships myself.

Behind a closed door, people in bathrooms have always found themselves alone with their thoughts. In water closets dating all the way back to ancient Rome, you could find little scribbles on the wall, someone's written name, or some crude message someone wrote while sitting and ridding the body of waste. The bathroom, because of its enclosure, has been the subject of all sorts of inscription and exclamation. "Albert was here, 2005" or rants of provocation and intolerance have existed in water closets as long as we've had them. In this isolation, faced with the corporeal reality of our own bodies' functions, the mind can imagine its limitations and its liberations. Privacy allows for private thoughts.

The writer Gcina Mhlophe, in her story "The Toilet," writes about a girl in Apartheid South Africa and how she found a sense of liberation and isolation in the public toilet. She could lock the door, be by herself, unmonitored, and unmolested, and write her chosen form of liberation and resistance. But it was a cautionary tale. The bathroom was also a space used to separate and divide during Apartheid. Public restrooms were sites of power and humiliation. "Whites only" separation revealed a clear hierarchy of racial status through spaces that were meant to serve a basic public, most human need. The unmaintained, unmanaged spaces for "non-whites" were often and predictably left filthy and without maintenance, reinforcing the inequalities and power of the state-sanctioned racial separation. It was as if the indignity and filth of public architecture had become a weapon to subjugate and divide, as well as to heal and protect. And yet, as in Soho and Port-au-Prince, it is that very waste, if unmanaged, that will spread illness without regard for class or race or status. The latrine unsheathes all these social complexities.

From the perspective of an architect, the concept of "modernity" brims with the lessons learned from almost two centuries of proof: structures equipped with potable water and flush toilets will protect public health. However, that vision was far from the reality for much of the world. Comprehensive access to these essential services is still lacking, even in many of the most rapidly growing metropolises of the world—economy pushing ahead of humanity.

Take the fastest-growing cities in the world—be it Dhaka, Kinshasa, Lagos, or many other global cities expected to exponentially urbanize in the next fifty years. The development of essential sanitation infrastructure lags dangerously behind the pace of urbanization in all these metropolises. Resources, both financial and human, are aligned toward commerce and finance rather than the lived experience of those expected to stoke the fires of profit. And existing structures stand no chance of accommodating the dreamed-upon futures of these cities without substantial interventions.

But international aid efforts often fall short of addressing this imbalance between the appetites of commerce and the realities of humanity—particularly in sanitation. And postcrisis interventions tend to prioritize immediate needs like food, shelter, and disease outbreak control. Physical water, sanitation, and hygiene (WASH) systems, though critical, frequently become secondary to the pressing visible concerns. The long-term (and often disruptive) planning, cost, and "unseen" nature of sanitation networks leave them so often pushed ahead to address another day.

Old Port-au-Prince was a planned city, laid out in a grid in parts, with sewers that ran beneath the cobblestone streets, connecting homes and businesses to an urban network. Those old neighborhoods of gingerbread houses still stood as a testament to the city's architectural legacy, and the neighborhoods containing them showed a sense of coherence, of planning, and—although the infrastructure is now aged and overburdened—an era when the city's expansion was still manageable.

This orderly grid gave way as the city expanded. The newer

neighborhoods, hastily built on the water's edge or in sprawling, informally arranged neighborhoods inhabited by the lower-income populations, were vastly different from the planned central downtown. Here, land was hastily filled in to accommodate an ever growing population, and settlements stretched across hillsides. These areas were neither planned nor connected to the city's infrastructure. No pipes ran beneath the streets to carry sewage or bring water. Often built by the residents themselves, these dense neighborhoods were places of ingenuity and survival but devoid of the hard systems necessary for a contemporary city equipped to handle any outbreak.

Port-au-Prince, originally designed for roughly two million residents, now houses somewhere between four and five million. These realities are sobering, but not unlike many other cities strained by population the world over. However, what *is* unique about Port-au-Prince is its historical entanglement with foreign aid, particularly from the United States.

In the 1950s, as part of a broader US development strategy in the region, aid flowed into Haiti to modernize key urban sectors. Boulevard Harry Truman, a grand thoroughfare, named in honor of the US president, stretches along the port and was designed to streamline the movement of goods and people and, in theory, to open up new economic possibilities for the capital. Yet, like much of the foreign aid that followed, it represented a top-down development model, often disconnected from the actual needs of the city's rapidly growing and marginalized populations.

Boulevard Harry Truman now marks a boundary between two vastly different worlds within the city. On one side, the crumbling remnants of downtown Port-au-Prince, where imperial-era sewers once ran beneath the streets and connected a smaller, more contained population. On the other, the sprawling districts of today's

Port-au-Prince, informal cities where open wastewater runs through makeshift systems reflect the absence of municipal oversight. This street, once a symbol of progress, now divides a city grappling with how to provide for millions living without access to clean water or sanitation.

What could be done given the limited resources available that would still have a significant impact? Dr. Pape wanted a new clinic, protected from the urban conditions outside its walls but also from the contaminated water threatening to invade. The clinic couldn't rely on external systems vulnerable to the old, unregulated sewage systems anymore, he reminded us. It had to be self-sustaining.

———

"If we can't trust the grid, let's make it off-grid," we suggested. We'd build a self-sustaining, self-supporting clinic that cleansed itself. To do so might not only protect patients here but also create a model that could be replicated across the city, potentially breaking the back of the epidemic.

"We can't let it get into the groundwater," Pape said gravely. If allowed to fully infiltrate the water systems, cholera threatened to become endemic and remain in Haiti forever—an unfixable and accepted fact of life.

Our team quickly set up locally, hiring architects to manage the construction, including Adam Saltzman, one of Eric Cesal's key recruits. David Saladik moved to Haiti to manage the new team and project. Our team needed many hands to take on this momentous project. We settled on a dual-purpose concept: to build a wastewater treatment plant and put the clinic on top.

For the first task, we enlisted help from civil engineers on designing a wastewater treatment system fit to meet a goal of cleaning

99.9 percent of any cholera bacteria in the water collected by the plant. The dual design called for a "wet building," like a public restroom, capable of collecting waste from patients while harvesting rainwater to constantly cleanse the facility. We designed a roof that funneled rainwater to the center rather than the sides so the building could manage its own water supply, with large water tanks positioned beneath.

The walls would be porous, with metal screens to allow a constant breeze, ensuring airflow while keeping odors from becoming overwhelming. This sacrificed some measure of privacy, but the patients in the throes of a pandemic, writhing in pain, dehydrated, and vomiting, needed constant rehydration and monitoring. They also needed to be visible to doctors at all times.

Labor and prefabrication also became critical components of our design. I wanted the construction process to benefit the local community, like it had in Butaro. Haiti is known for its intricate metalwork—artisans re-purpose old oil drums and scrap metal into ornamental artwork. We recruited local craftspeople to design a façade that would be both handmade and highly functional. Using wooden jigs, they punched large metal sheets into consistent forms, allowing for precise airflow while maintaining the building's aesthetic integrity. The result was a dynamic, high-tech structure created through local craftsmanship, a perfect fusion of innovation and tradition.

Dr. Pape had other forms of local support as well. He had established a program for sex workers—often the most vulnerable to HIV/AIDS—providing them with training and jobs. Many of them worked in a woodshop he installed on the clinic's campus, making furniture for the facility. Together, we designed and built the tables, chairs, and cabinetry using strong hardwoods and artisanal care.

And the structure was capped off by a contribution from one

of Haiti's most well-known painters, in the form of a mural at the clinic's entrance, thanking the donors and supporters who made the project possible.

This was LOFAB in practice. It wasn't about dismissing prefabrication or automation but about ensuring there was still space for the handmade and the human touch. The building became a testament to this approach—a structure that felt tangible, crafted by hands and deeply connected to its community.

When we painted it in patterns of blue, symbolizing the sky and sea beyond, the building seemed to come alive. Its beauty, its *venustas*, was unmistakable. It was strong—meant for more than just shelter, intended for the medium, if not long, term. It embodied *utilitas*, designed with a clear purpose: to provide safe, clean facilities in the face of a public health crisis.

But more than anything, it was a symbol of hope. A structure that signaled to the community of Cité de Dieu that their resilience, in spite of everything, could be honored through the spaces they inhabited.

As the walls and roof went up and patients began to enter the facility, I started to imagine what could be next—installing similar water stations throughout Cité de Dieu and other diarrheal disease centers. Just as Dr. Pape had created a visionary clinic in 1982 to address a global epidemic, he too had done the same for the epidemic scourge of 2011.

———

In international aid discussions, I spoke about public utilities as the first step in a new sanitation era. Our cities, strained by population growth and climate-related disaster, have become increasingly fragile ecosystems. We need resilient, reliable, and maintainable infrastructure—public utilities that handle water and waste effectively and do so for our health. And, I would argue, we need to make those elements—our hidden systems—more visible. Our urge is to make the "lesser" elements of our human condition "go away." Why don't we instead design these systems so we can see them, protect them, and ensure their longevity?

As architects, we're taught to think about buildings as individual entities, but the truth is, they're never separate from the broader built environment they sit within. They plug into a network, and that network determines how we live, how we function as a society. Everything we see is designed, but what we don't see is designed, too, and it shapes the way we live.

We need to reimagine our role as designers, not just of structures, but of systems. If we fail to do so, we'll continue to build places that, like Port-au-Prince, work for some but not for all.

Haiti also taught me that our structures should tread more lightly on the world around them, harnessing energy and managing waste and water independently. In doing so, we could reduce the burden on the environment and better protect the health of the people living within them.

As our world grows and faces challenges like pandemics and climate change, the question becomes: What kind of spaces do we deserve to live in? What rights do we have to clean air, clean water, and safe environments? By answering these questions, we begin to shape a future where our cities and buildings are designed not for survival alone, but for human dignity and health.

And by doing so, we don't just fight disease; we reclaim the right to breathe freely.

I couldn't help but think of my hometown, Poughkeepsie. Much like Port-au-Prince, it too was in need of renewal. And as if the past were tugging me home, an old friend reached out asking me to help with Poughkeepsie's failing infrastructure. This problem was due not to an earthquake, but to a hurricane that had swept through Poughkeepsie, swelled a northside creek, and flooded many of the surrounding buildings—including the school that my father had attended growing up. I was working in the midst of Haiti's devastation and once again my thoughts drifted to the challenges waiting for me back home.

Chapter 5

THE MALL

Hudson Valley, New York

I was surprised to see Brian Doyle's name unexpectedly show up in my inbox. He was the father of a high school buddy from back in Poughkeepsie. His messages were usually forwarded notes or scattered updates from home—a note on his latest project, a link to an article, words of encouragement from recent press I had received. But today's subject line, blunt and urgent, beckoned me:

"You've been spending all this time in Haiti and Rwanda rebuilding hard-hit places," he wrote, words brimming with a kind of brutal clarity. "We are struggling to recover from Hurricane Irene, which flooded the city and damaged our center. Now might be the time to come home."

I took a moment to sit on a bench and gather my thoughts. My work had taken me to some of the most distant corners of the world. And I'd watched projects change those places with speed. And yet Poughkeepsie seemed different somehow. A struggling place persistently just out of reach of renewal.

My mom, after a few years widowed, had remarried and decided to leave Poughkeepsie. She sold our house and moved closer to me in Massachusetts. I understood her desire to build anew somewhere else. But my brother and I felt gutted at the loss of our house, and I felt severed from my hometown and its lingering memories. That place had never felt farther away but now was calling out to me.

"Brian," I wrote back, "I'm actually in NYC taking some meetings. Could I take the train up tomorrow?"

———

The train to Poughkeepsie from Grand Central station brought back something visceral. Growing up, New York City had always been a promise. In middle school my father would take us to the St. Patrick's Day Parade or a Yankees game for the day. In high school, we would ride down on weekends to run around the city and race to make the last train back upstate after midnight. The tracks cradle the eastern side of the Hudson the whole way up. The left-side seats were the ones to get, facing north, watching the majestic Hudson reveal itself. I'd count the stops on the way up—Tarrytown, Ossining, Croton Harmon, Peekskill, Garrison, Cold Spring, Beacon. Poughkeepsie was the last and final, the end of the line. It felt that way for a lot of reasons.

Poughkeepsie station sat between two bridges, which soared overhead as I met Brian and we took off to walk along Main Street, past once-vibrant buildings now faded and boarded up, their windows empty.

"Why did they abandon a place with so much potential, so many resources?" I asked, shaking my head. I knew many had already tried and failed to turn this place around. That call to change something, and the knowledge that Poughkeepsie had shaken off attempts to do so, felt overwhelming. It was the call and the curse of the architect. Change is possible and hubris is destructive. But who could think the next effort in this place would be any different?

When my family moved to Poughkeepsie in 1991, I was eleven years old. It was not my parents' first choice. My father grew up about fifteen miles east, in a small village called Millbrook. But he'd gone to high school in Poughkeepsie, at the time when it was the commercial shopping center of Dutchess County.

But now the downtown district on Main Street was bereft, with vacant storefronts and a large population of people living on the street. Main Street had been bricked over to make a pedestrian mall in the 1970s as part of an urban renewal plan. By the 1990s, it looked decrepit and empty. Two three-lane highways ringed Main Street and isolated the center city into a sort of island surrounded by highways. Historic buildings went unmaintained and were ultimately demolished. As too were front lawns and the trees contained within them. Large surface parking lots were all that remained between Main Street and the highways on either side. The result was a scary and desolate city center.

When Brian and I took a walk along Main Street, there were, however, a few signs of life—or at least potential—still lingering. The street stretched from west to east, passing through ten blocks of patchwork businesses. At the intersection of Market Street, the city's nerve center rose up: county offices, the courthouse, and the Bardavon Opera House, in operation since 1869. These icons were relics of another era that the city couldn't quite carry forward. When we turned north on Hamilton Street, we faced the broad, gray expanse of the same arterial highway, a three-lane barrier we had to pass to leave the island core. We passed four sprawling parking lots, reminders of old urban renewal plans that had never quite panned out.

I saw the highway and surface parking lots in a different way than I had as a youth growing up there. In high school it was a wasteland, a field of pavement that felt like nothing had ever grown there. But to me, trained now to see the marks of 1960s planning, it was clearer.

The roads had taken out old buildings and smaller streets. Grand houses were too close to the highway. There must have been trees and lawns there. The road was large and created a dead-end street on either side; they must have connected through when this highway was just a two-lane city road. Now that highway was a boundary that divided the city into separate quadrants from north to south and east to west. The historic train station on the river was once connected to the downtown; now it was divided. The north and south sides were once woven together in a fabric of streets and buildings, town houses and businesses. Now it was one main street with vast amounts of surface parking and oversized highways surrounding the entirety of the city center. And at the center was the mall.

This was the legacy of urban renewal. In architecture school we had been taught that "urban renewal" stood in for a set of top-down, overarching planning moves in the 1960s and '70s that destroyed many cities across the United States. They were often racist (a method of "Negro removal," as James Baldwin once put it) and intended to displace poor people, we were told, center cars, and gash cities with scars that drained urban environments of their identities and life-bloods.

"This used to be the heart of the city. This was a mill pond where factories started," Brian said. "And this"—he nodded toward the cracked pavement—"was where people gathered, where businesses thrived." Now it's a five-way interchange with nothing but pavement.

There were no signs of that pond remaining, no hint of the natural world that had once defined this place. Between the eastern and western byways, there were as many low, long, flat parking lots as there were buildings.

"The creek's still here," he said, "just hidden under the road."

The waterway had been siphoned into a concrete channel to make way for the highway in the 1960s, Brian explained. But nature didn't care much about those channels. Basements of businesses and homes nearby were all flooded out when storms came through.

A small creek ran beneath us—though the word *ran* was generous. "See how high the creek rose?" Brian gestured to the edge of the bridge. Branches were backed up against the concrete channel where water surged, fighting against the embankments. Nature trying to find a way.

We crossed the arterial highway, leaving the asphalt island behind as the surroundings softened into old neighborhoods. Brian's office came into view—an aging brick building that had once housed the Catholic school in the city. "This was Poughkeepsie's first high school when it was built in the early 1900s," Brian explained. It changed ownership to Our Lady of Lourdes Catholic school in the 1950s, when they built the new public Poughkeepsie High, which Brian's son Daniel and I attended.

A jolt of "duh" hit me while staring up at the worn bricks and stoic windows. My father went to Lourdes for high school in the 1960s, and it was just registering with me that he spent every school day walking these blocks at the same time they were demolishing the houses around it.

The building, weathered and tired, held echoes of that past, but the years hadn't been kind. It wore the signs of deferred maintenance, a structure barely holding on through the hollowing out of the city's tax base.

"The storm damage might get us some federal support, and we need a plan to make it work," Brian informed me, finally letting on to why he'd compelled me here. "This is where we could use your help."

I felt the opportunity and gravity of it. Plans can be drawn, sure, the holes can be plugged, but what about these bigger issues—the creek, the highways, the sea of parking? These were infrastructural problems that required big investments in federal and state dollars to change. The issues here were deep and systemic and expensive. An architecture and design firm can stop the bleeding, but what about the structural conditions that brought us here in the first place? Then I thought of Haiti, where a horrific event had stirred up the action and energy that had been latent.

Ironically, the highways and demolition were once seen as Poughkeepsie's bright future. They were imagined to renew the city center. Growing up here, I had heard that architects and planners had killed the city, but my new perch as a practitioner gave me a more nuanced view. What was it that made this place so difficult to change? I wondered.

In the shadows of the buildings, I looked back at the arterial slicing through the city, a constant reminder of decisions made long ago. So much money was spent here to set the stage for rebirth and that promised prosperity but left only fractures. I'd need to understand those choices fully—the past that held Poughkeepsie in its grip.

———

Robert Levine was a local lawyer and family friend who also sat on the city's planning commission. He agreed to meet me for a drink and looked at me over the glass. "That was a time for big ideas," he said. "PURA, the Poughkeepsie Urban Renewal Agency. They set it up to coalesce the federal infrastructure dollars and get the city as much money as possible. In that way, they were successful." Poughkeepsie was one of only 150 "Model Cities" nationally that got special funding to address poverty, housing, racial inequity, and basic infrastructure.

"I was taught that urban renewal was all about removing poor people and taking their land," I said.

"That certainly happened in places. But remember, Lyndon Johnson's federal program was an anti-poverty program, too. The irony is demolition was supported by both the right and the left. The right wanted to clear away blighted spaces, and the left wanted modern housing, but they both agreed, these buildings had to go."

"The road to hell is paved with good intentions," I muttered.

He looked at me like a teacher.

"The city had a unique window to get this money. They needed plans developed fast, and they needed political buy-in. They hoped change would come."

He then pulled out a manila folder from his briefcase. "I brought this for you," he said, and opened it. Inside was an old paper-bound booklet . The book had an aerial map of Poughkeepsie on the front with a red filter wash over it, and the letters *PURA* written in bold, sans serif font, on all the documents. "This was the plan. I wanted you to see it."

The old planning documents were fascinating. Maps and sketches of the city Poughkeepsie would be. A central business district was imagined with a new civic core that included a city hall and convention center. Street-level renderings and perspective drawings envisioned a beautiful, lively, tree-lined street. I saw the tools and sleight of hand of my chosen trade.

Demolition of "blight" in graphic overlays of red hatch marks, as if nothing existed there. Parking was needed and space for the highways that would surround the center city, where Main Street buildings would be preserved but the street bricked into a pedestrian mall. The vision of the mall would bring people back to the city and would compete with the suburban malls being built all over the country at that time and farther down the highway from Poughkeepsie, five miles south.

The pedestrian mall plan had worked elsewhere, in Kalamazoo, Michigan, and Ithaca, New York, so Poughkeepsie representatives wanted those same ideas here, he told me. They visited Kalamazoo to see what had worked and could be replicated.

Many cities faced this same dilemma in the mid-1950s and '60s. From the passing of the Federal-Aid Highway Act to the Great Society legislation of 1965, American cities saw their biggest transformational population shift in history. There were overlapping federal reasons for the decay of cities across America: unanticipated side effects of legislation, the deferred depreciation tax laws around property, increased racial division and segregation, red-lining of urban zones made unavailable for mortgages and forcing condensed urban concentrations of poverty, the perception of blight, the actuality of decrepit and poorly maintained buildings and streets in urban centers, and, of course, the flight of residents to new suburban rings of the cities they once occupied, surrounded by new strip malls and shopping malls.

In 1972, it appeared that Kalamazoo had turned a decaying town into a thriving core. Kalamazoo's gleaming revitalization beckoned, and forty-two representatives from Poughkeepsie flew to Michigan to tour the results and meet the head of the architecture and planning team responsible, Victor Gruen.

———

Gruen's solution, the pedestrian mall, seemed straightforward. Replicate the attraction of the suburban mall, but do it in the historic main street corridor and bring people back to the city center. To do this, they needed to take the cars away and close the main street, then create ample parking for people to make it a destination. He proposed to take the decrepit buildings down and replace them with surface parking lots.

Gruen knew that malls could work. He was the original designer of the Southdale Shopping Center, America's first enclosed, air-conditioned mall, in Edina, Minnesota. He had built a career around dropping shopping centers onto the outskirts of nearly every metropolitan center in America. In one assessment from *The New Yorker*, Gruen "may well have been the most influential architect of the twentieth century."

In school, I had heard of Gruen's reputation. It was a mixed legacy. The mall was looked down upon as a form of commodity-driven architecture. Gruen was talked about as an innovator with the mall typology, but that typology had also destroyed cities and towns and main streets the country over. Often, he proposed mixed-use development that never came to be, and main streets suffered even as malls, while successful businesses were also precarious. Gruen's plan to save main streets needed to attract shops and pedestrians back to the urban core with anchor businesses. He wanted to take the best of the suburban mall and the best of main street and merge them. That is what he proposed for Poughkeepsie.

There were creative ideas in this plan about walkability and pedestrian-centered experiences. I had recently visited the new Times Square in NYC, which had closed to traffic to reduce cars, not unlike the plan in Robert's book from fifty years ago. But the key difference in Poughkeepsie was that the planned demolition took place without the promised future development ever following. The plan had five key points:

Phase one was adding new highways to "solve" traffic. Two new three-lane highways—running perpendicular from the Hudson River—would feed into and away from the mid-Hudson bridge and bypass Main Street downtown. A third major highway would elevate connecting towns north and south. Parallel was Main Street, which the new roads bypassed and encircled, leaving an island at the center. The roads were like moats. The highways were sized for a future three times the size, with 100,000 cars streaming through the city a day. This projection proved to be a reach. Fifty years later, this number had risen to an average of only 25,000 or so.

Second was demolition. Roads were expanded, old nineteenth-century buildings made way for parking on the backside of Main Street, "blighted" buildings turned into oceans of asphalt. Easy access was the claim, but in practice, what was left was a city made for parking. The expanding boundary of the highway as a speed thoroughfare made it even less attractive for people to cross it, further distancing residences from interacting with the core business district.

Third was the creation of new civic amenities like a new city hall and new civic convention center and hotel. Large plots dominated by brutalist buildings were set back from the street.

Fourth was to turn Main Street into a bricked-over pedestrian mall filled with planters and benches, becoming a walkable district for pedestrian traffic only.

The fifth phase, the one that was so crucial to making phases one through four work, was where the city would be repaired after all this supposed rejuvenation. The people would move back into the downtown, and hope would be restored. Population would boom, and new business markets would benefit to inspire a thriving renewed city. This, unfortunately, never came to fruition.

———

So if, regrettably, architects and planners bulldozed this city, how could we avoid repeating the mistakes of the past?

I remembered Paul Farmer's words again. If we believe in the work, he told me, and believe progress to be possible even with the short windows afforded by political pressure, we have to jump at the chance. Sitting idly by was not an option.

———

"Your father and mine had the same ambition when he came here," Robert said to me over a quiet dinner one night. "This is a relay race, not a sprint. We have to plant the seeds for growth, attract business to stay here, build better housing for people so they want to live here."

This larger goal wouldn't stop at the plans we'd made already. The schools would need to improve, so the city could attract young families again. Downtown businesses needed a thriving Main Street, so people would again be working, living, and using the city for more than resource extraction. In short, this place needed to become a full-fledged home.

Poughkeepsie had lost generations of people to other places. We needed to do the work that would bring those lost sons and daughters back to the place that raised them. Robert wasn't just making a pitch for redevelopment, he was making a pitch to me, too.

———

In both Rwanda and Haiti, I'd encountered similar hunger to retain talent and encourage people to invest in the places that reared them. Development jargon calls the problem "brain drain," but the larger point about opportunity ladders is relevant in every community.

One lesson I took from Partners In Health was the value of genuine rootedness: They didn't just "fly in" to provide aid—they lived in the communities they served. I picked up the value of this model and immersed myself as well. In Rwanda, I stayed on the hill with doctors, working on-site during construction. In Haiti, we built a team who lived day to day within the complexities of that place. We set up an office, assembled a local team, and started a flywheel that kept turning.

Immersion was central to my practice. "Helicopter architecture" that so often imposed cookie-cutter solutions from one place onto another was a valid critique of the urban renewal era. It fostered mistrust and pushback on efforts to rebuild and improve communities in need.

In the US in the 1960s, writers like Jane Jacobs argued that her neighborhood of the West Village in Manhattan and others deserved to be saved from the demolishing efforts of Robert Moses and his highway plans for New York City. Jacobs's efforts, among others in the Hudson Valley like the nonprofit Scenic Hudson, inspired national activism and resistance efforts around federal infrastructure projects that ended the urban renewal era. And in the wake of that, environmental and historic preservation laws and community design centers popped up to provide more pathways to citizen self-determination in the 1970s and '80s.

That famous David vs. Goliath battle of the urban renewal era was written about in *The Power Broker*, by Robert Caro, his biography of Robert Moses and his work building much of the region around New York City's parks, housing, public spaces, and highways. Caro wrestles with the conundrum and contradictions of Moses. Those of someone who could envision and make happen the largest infrastructure projects in the state—like Long Island's Jones Beach and the Triborough Bridge—but also fall prey to the shortsightedness of a car-based urbanism, which prioritized highways over historic street grids and structures. I'd encountered it through my father's first edition, dog-eared copy on my shelf, with its tattered, taped-together jacket. On my way to architecture school, I decided it was time to finally dig in and quickly understood why it was my father's favorite book.

———

Moses is, of course, a complicated figure, and the book fit in with the conflicted feeling I was trying to grapple with in Poughkeepsie. The stories of resistance to Moses sank in and supported my instinctual aversion to unfettered new development. But after fifty years of stifled growth and decay in Poughkeepsie (and other towns like it), I was also aware of a community yearning for the kind of bold, visionary, and large-scale systems thinking that could reshape a place in the ways Moses had in his early career. Why was it that Shanghai, for example, was able to build over 500 miles of subway in the past thirty years, while in the same period New York City built 3.5 miles? It seemed to me the correct answer to this was somewhere in the middle. What if we took the negative and sometimes positive lessons from the last great federal infrastructure era of the 1960s and applied them today with our current understanding of how cities grow and are shaped by design?

"Renewal" needed a balance of local action and broad vision. Sitting with Robert helped me understand this wasn't just about good versus evil, progressives versus traditionalists. Vision might turn up funding, but real solutions also demand political pragmatism. It was messy work, but I'd seen change under more difficult circumstances. Why not in my hometown?

I still hesitated, wary of adding one more stone to the well-paved road of good intentions. A few weeks later, a colleague named John Rudikoff—who also grew up in Poughkeepsie—took that train ride up to meet me on Main Street and asked the same questions I had. I now had a pitch for our team and funders.

What if we set up a local office, a newer version of the community design centers of the 1970s? We could establish a presence on Main Street and foster real dialogue about the issues people felt were critical to getting Poughkeepsie off and running again.

We needed to start planning from the bottom up, long before any federal funds would arrive. That way, when—honestly, more like if—funding appeared, these projects would be vetted, community-supported, and shovel-ready. The place to start, incidentally, was at that downtrodden downtown mall.

———

Robert connected me with Eric Baxter, whose father had been my high school shop teacher and who made a second career for himself as a real estate developer in town. Eric had entered development as well and now wanted to commit fully to revitalizing Poughkeepsie's downtown. "I have a few projects that could use your help," he told me.

Eric pointed out a striking cast-iron building on Main Street, three stories tall, its pediment proudly marked "Built in 1876." Lined on both sides by other tall, historic buildings, it was a beautiful specimen that spoke to a grander, more industrial time of a thriving city with a dense street grid, tall and abundant buildings, and a robust economy. It looked like the kinds of structures that line the streets of New York City's SoHo district. The kind of place that made you understand why Jane Jacobs had fought so hard for preservation. I was glad they were still standing. "That one?" I asked, intrigued. He shook his head. "Not the cast iron. That's empty and off the market. I mean that one next to it, the ugly brick building."

Ugly was right. It was a boxy, two-story structure with small windows. Probably the least attractive building on the block, maybe in the whole town. "But imagine it with apartments and new offices," Eric said, "and a design firm on the ground floor that we could build together."

I started imagining the design office as a space for collaboration, a hub for creative energy that would also make us part of a new Main Street corridor. We'd be as invested in the success of this place as one could ever be, working there and subject to the same disruptions to everyday life we'd ask the people of Poughkeepsie to tolerate. Eric was offering me the chance to make that vision real—true building from the ground up—and we'd have control over the design. "It just needs to be fast and affordable," he added.

The building didn't have any historical significance, but its open steel frame offered long, flexible spans, perfect for creative design. We could add a few apartments on top, creating live-work spaces, and it was positioned at the heart of a historic stretch downtown. It could be an anchor for revitalizing Main Street, block by block.

Eric still had a few other projects in mind. "There's a cluster of buildings over on the corner of the arterial and Hamilton," he said, "and I have thoughts on some housing options just a few blocks away."

He had already transformed an old mill building, once a struggling Chinese restaurant, into the downtown's most popular pub. Now Eric wanted to do the same for more properties. He'd already proven the potential to turn something left behind into something vibrant and beautiful.

"We need people that care about this place to come home and invest in it," he said, leaning forward. "My sister and I want to double down on Poughkeepsie." This was being shared from a developer's perspective, but I could see how elemental it was to the downtown core. Without the economic base and committed commercial tenants and investors willing to support them, no city center, no downtown mall would thrive. Eric and his family were taking a big risk, and I appreciated his optimism.

"A relay race," I said, thinking of how following in a father's footsteps could shape a path forward. This felt like the right chance to take—one that carried a real sense of responsibility, ownership, and partnership.

———

My team and I set up a temporary office as we worked on the plans for a new one. Just being on Main Street, proximate to the revitalization around us, began to bring more people through the door. A local affordable housing nonprofit developer, Hudson River Housing (HRH), had been the only game in town, buying buildings and putting assisted living and subsidized housing throughout the city center. They had made a big bet on an old factory farther up Main Street and renovated it into new artist studios and a new community café. Their next project was an old barn that once housed the trolleys that came up and down Main, and they wanted to work alongside us, too.

HRH, and their thoughtful program officer Elizabeth Celaya, wanted to create an art and event space, with a proper gallery for the community that would also highlight an incredible building hiding in plain sight. The Trolley Barn Gallery, a simple historic renovation, would turn out to be our first completed building in the United States.

Another partner, Ned Sullivan of Scenic Hudson, came on board. Scenic Hudson had been saving and protecting Hudson River waterfront for the last fifty years and was looking to extend their responsibilities to the cities and people who relied on that waterfront as their lifeblood. Scenic Hudson had been looking all over Hudson Valley towns for a place to move, and after a planning study I made the case to their board to take over an abandoned factory in Poughkeepsie's northside. The old Gage Factory on Parker Avenue had been sitting abandoned for years. It had amazing bones and could be an anchor for the northside of Poughkeepsie—which needed it. It sat on the Fall Kill Creek and was adjacent to a new walkway over the Hudson, which was drawing tourists. Getting an anchor nonprofit to renovate and commit to this large project would be a boon to the city and help its broader ambitions, but it would take some convincing.

———

These old factories, built before air-conditioning, had large windows for light and air ventilation. Like the hospitals of the nineteenth century, the climate and its permeability were essential to making the building function. But most of these windows had been bricked in over time. Looking at the Gage Factory's façade, I could see the header, the frame of the old window, still there, just waiting to be opened up again to the world. I knew new light and ventilation would reawaken the building, just like I'd seen in Rwanda. Buildings needed to breathe, and here, with a unique design touch, we could make this one breathe all year round, creating natural ventilation even in the winter months by placing small heating and cooling coils below each window. This way, the window could be reopened and grand, while giving some level of control back to the people gathering inside.

Practices that were once common but now lost to supposed convenience and technological advances emerged innovative and new as we rethought the old factory for this updated office space function. What if we could restore a building into a healthy office facility that could generate fresh air, produce its own energy, and awaken a corner of the city. For fifty years, Scenic Hudson had been protecting and reimagining the environmental assets around us. What if they did the same with the built environment assets we live amid? It was a reminder of the value in the discarded things around us. The board was sold, and acquisition, design, and construction commenced—allowing our nascent office to stabilize and grow.

A NEW SIX-POINT PLAN

A few dips into the local commercial market helped, but systemic hurdles still presented a tremendous obstacle to Poughkeepsie and other cities like it. A city could *look* renovated, with cute businesses setting up shop and trying to get a foothold, but the guts of Poughkeepsie still needed a helping hand. Transportation was in need of help, health-care needs were not being met, and the schools were not in shape to attract young families who'd bring their skills and energy to bear on the community.

In Rwanda I'd seen that holistic attention was required to make change. Paul Farmer taught that we needed to be systems designers and take responsibility for everything our work touched. It was not okay to put in our hours, call it a job done, and move on. Every brick laid and every ask made of government had network effects on everything around it.

I drew a Venn diagram of three central concerns—perception, imagination, and mobility—the big things that needed to change, and where I, as a designer, could complete, influence, or encourage these changes. I started thinking at a more urban level, like Gruen did, but without limiting myself to anticipated pushback from protectors of the status quo. I needed to become a do-whatever-it-takes tactician. Regardless, we needed a legible plan, with delineated steps, that could allow others to join us in chipping away at the bigger structural issues.

One: Perceptions needed to change

Poughkeepsie had become a negative conversation point, a history charged with decay and decades of poverty. It had to have a better story to tell about itself, from the outside and from the inside. Perception is pride of place and a shared sense of dignity that values people above all.

Here, architects can make a big impact. Images, development, and visualizations of the future can all point toward a brighter, more hopeful tomorrow. And while those same images can be weaponized, they are also necessary to imagine the new and build enthusiasm for change.

So we set about sharing some spruced-up conceptual ideas of empty spaces built anew. Surface lots needed to be reimagined as potential sites of development, the fabric of the city needed to be restitched together by filling in open pockets of underbuilt land

and shuttered businesses, the operational parts of the city needed to move closer to the edge of the roads instead of set back behind parking, parking had to be pulled away from pedestrian life and placed behind buildings or in the center of blocks to let humans take precedent again, and key anchor buildings needed to be given fresh life.

Two: We needed to reimagine the public realm

Growing up, Poughkeepsie was known for an elevated train bridge that crossed the Hudson and loomed large. It had been unused since the 1970s, a beacon of commercial change and economic decline. And it was overbuilt in order to carry freight trains across the river in the late 1800s.

Inspired by the High Line in New York City, a local nonprofit wanted to convert the bridge into a pedestrian walkway over the Hudson. The Dyson Foundation, led by Robert Dyson—a friend of my father's from growing up in Millbrook—had committed seed capital to complete it by the time I was setting up shop on Main Street, and it had begun to bring bikers, runners, and walkers to the city. It functioned as a kind of proof of concept for how liabilities could be rethought into assets. On both sides of the river, running and biking trails connected small eastern and western river cities without a reliance on cars. Planning efforts on the northside could capitalize on that investment to extend opportunities for visitors to stay, spend, and reimagine the city.

The Hurricane Irene–induced flooding of the Fall Kill Creek that brought me back to Poughkeepsie was the most obvious place to start thinking about stitching the city back together with green corridors to protect against stormwater surges and provide new open space. A "Daylighting" movement had taken hold in other cities, a trend toward taking out the old culverts and breaking down the old concrete walls to allow the creek waters to surge naturally with the landscape. This strategy would help both create new walkable amenities and protect against flood surges as climate change advanced. In Poughkeepsie, opening up the creek would mean creating parklets along its circuitous curvy run through the city. Certain sections that had been paved over would be reopened to bridges and green space, and a new public path that lined the creek would need local business to reorient themselves and create new central entrances that would bleed out into the shared plaza. We worked on rendering and visualizing this to attract grants and partnerships to make this happen, one park at a time.

Three: We needed to revolutionize mobility in the region

Car-based 1960s urbanism had done untold damage to Poughkeepsie. Insisting that parking lots and big highways were necessary for a future city had left Poughkeepsie with swaths of both unused and unusable land. A parking study showed that even when demand peaked during the day, only 50 percent of parking spaces were used. Parking is always tough in urban revitalization conditions, because drivers see traffic and delays to their point-to-point experiences from home to work to commerce as the primary burdens on their daily interactions with shared space. But the counterpoint is to raise the question of what we are all willing to sacrifice to make driving as frictionless as possible.

While an inconvenience to driving into downtown may sacrifice a few extra minutes, failure to "right-size" highways and parking space not only inconveniences and delays pedestrians but also chokes out precisely the commercial activity needed to raise up a community and service those roads and spaces.

In New York City, under Michael Bloomberg's administration, Janette Sadik-Khan as commissioner of transportation (between 2007 and 2013) led a project to reimagine streets and give unused land over to public use. They called them "road diets" because they shrunk the big, oversized highways into multimodal public streets that made walking and biking safer, while restricting movement for trucks and delivery. It was working throughout New York City. Why not deploy them in Poughkeepsie? Roads are public spaces, so we should treat them like they are the public's, not the private driver of the car moving through the city.

Later, during the Biden administration (2020–2024) and the debate over its landmark Bipartisan Infrastructure Bill (2021), federal administrators included a Reconnecting Communities Pilot to use federal dollars to fund projects that undo harm from twentieth-century infrastructure and highway projects that had, like in Poughkeepsie, broken up social spheres, harmed pedestrian livability, or created deep fractures between "haves" and "have-nots" in local communities. We needed to reduce arterial highways and city roads and we waited on studies to show why.

Four: We needed to expand ownership in homes and businesses

Poughkeepsie had fallen into a strange budgetary problem as the city decayed throughout the twentieth and early twenty-first centuries; they were reliant on tax liens paid by foreclosed property owners. Large conglomerates search for foreclosures around the country and buy them at fire sale prices, paying off the liens but then holding property without management. These become something referred to colloquially as "zombie properties." The zombies tend to be held by landlords living far away from the places where the properties are located. The residents of these buildings tended to be selected for their vulnerability and lack of resources to demand better conditions and treatment from the property owners, and without tenant pressures, there are few incentives to improve these properties or the lands surrounding them. Poughkeepsie's northside, which was mostly made up of modest, single-family homes, was littered with these zombie properties.

A potential solution existed in a town just across the river called Newburgh, where a nonprofit land bank had been set up to absorb foreclosures and then use the properties as collateral to renovate, redistribute, or invest in with third-party dollars. After public pressure and advocacy, local city council members used recently approved legislation to set up the land bank, paving the way toward more local control and ownership of these foreclosed "zombie" assets.

Five: We needed to build a pressure campaign that encouraged anchor institutions to reinvest in the center city

Poughkeepsie was central to a number of universities such as Vassar College, Marist College, Dutchess Community College, and the Culinary Institute of America—to invest in the center city by placing institutional buildings downtown. In Worcester, Massachusetts, a city that had much in common with Poughkeepsie's economic history, colleges were encouraged to build student housing and campus buildings in the central business district. This attracted commercial activity like restaurants and bars and other amenities that were both an economic engine and a boon to creative reimagination of the city itself. But at the same time, it also better integrated the student population into the community. This decreased social frictions typical to college enclaves situated within populated areas, while also encouraging the universities to commit to security infrastructure that simultaneously benefited students, local residents, and businesses. Poughkeepsie is still pushing for this investment of capital and security from the local universities, but as a goal it remains one of the single most impactful changes that can be carried out by the community around a distressed population center.

Six: We needed to transform Poughkeepsie's schools

That remained far outside my expertise. Gerry Laybourne, a regional resident and philanthropist, set up a nonprofit called DAY ONE that took the lead to target early childhood education. If a community could become best in class in early childhood, it could show young families a city on the rise. We worked with Gerry on the development of her center, and she set up offices in our building on Main Street.

Another education expert, Rob Watson (a Poughkeepsie high school graduate and product of the Harvard Graduate School of Education), was working closely with us to put nationally productive interventions to work on the local school district.

Now we had a surfeit of ideas and passion, but the ultimate question would always be how to attach those plans to sufficient funding mechanisms. We would need to identify which of these points could attract government (largely federal) dollars, which could draw investment from the business sector, and which would need to be catalyzed by philanthropy.

What was the architect's role then? Was it to draw plans or visualize images? Or was it like I was seeing in Poughkeepsie, to be more of a connector between the government, social, and private sectors. I felt like a matchmaker or a producer of a large movie, instead of an artisan erasing aberrant pencil lines. But the future city, in all its grandeur, with all its characters and potential, came into view.

———

Lasting design work is by nature slow, iterative, and time-consuming. But not necessarily because of the labor and machinery needed to convert ideas into physical structures. Lasting work requires outreach and playback, listening and responding to the people, which so often becomes the first cut for faceless conglomerates practicing a more hands-off version of the practice. The work I found myself doing in Poughkeepsie reminded me more of efforts like those my father had taken on as a public servant when he was a commissioner of public works and needed to cross political lines and sticky budgetary concerns to marshal resources that would hold up to public scrutiny. We'd happened upon work that required a higher standard of care than typically contemplated in the private design sector with clients who were amorphous and broad—a public.

Some of these lessons were national ones. Cities are constantly in a state of renewal, revitalization, and reimagination. They need architects and planners to assist in the vision work, to be between the community, the client, and the codes to make it real. And often those visions are necessary to unlock capital to pay for them, be it federal, state, private, or philanthropic funding. And the elements of this six-point plan—perception change, public realm reimagination, right-sized safe mobility, distributed property ownership, engaged anchor institutions, and supported schools—could themselves be applied to many (struggling) cities in America. Just with differing levels of emphasis and stages.

The goals are all ultimately the same, to make places that are thriving, healthy, and abundant, where people can live, work, and amenities like school, recreation, and community are broadly available.

Poughkeepsie had gotten a second life in the 1950s, when IBM chose to make its mainframe computers there. It was an economic engine of the region, a huge win, and an opportunity to bring brilliant minds and capital to the area. But the outsized and specific nature of the IBM boom also invited precarity, a single-source fragility that urban renewal misdiagnosed and could not fix. Without creative long-term planning, it invited sprawl and drew people away from, rather than toward, the city center. It created suburban rings that largely had no need to interact with the downtown, where the vast majority of the populace needed the activity most.

All across America, there were places like Poughkeepsie—cities that had seen large-scale urban renewal funding, suffered substantial population decline, witnessed the collapse of their main streets, and experimented with pedestrian (or suburban) malls to revive their commercial centers. My team identified over a hundred cities with similar stories, including Easton, Erie, and Wilkes-Barre in Pennsylvania; Worcester and Holyoke in Massachusetts; Saginaw in Michigan; and Wheeling, West Virginia.

Establishing design offices in each wasn't realistic. But there was potential in the model as a future blueprint for design practice. When young people in lectures asked my vision of a successful future in the industry, I would tell them, "Go back to your hometown, wherever it is—a place where you have social ties and a network. Don't wait for commissions the traditional way—that's passive. Instead, create your own opportunities, embedded in a community that already trusts you. You'll have a much more direct impact and likely grow faster as a designer."

I encouraged a "locatect" mindset, making a difference where they're rooted and connecting with one another across regions. This grassroots approach, I believed, would yield a stronger collective impact than the top-down "starchitect" model. If we plant a thousand seeds, who knows what will emerge to inspire the world with innovative approaches to revitalization.

Revisiting Gruen and his work designing pedestrian and suburban malls around the country and world, he often designed these centers with large rings of housing and entertainment that would fill the parking lots and create multiuse residential and commercial centers to support them. He went on to bemoan how few of those residential complexes followed through on the full plan for the malls, leaving these complexes and cities fragile and empty. My mind was opening a bit, shifting beyond the entrenched idea these big planners had brought only devastation—be they Gruen in Poughkeepsie or Robert Moses in New York City—to what Robert Levine had asked me to imagine these city makers as systemic thinkers in a long relay race of urban evolution. I wondered what was possible if, with the right energy and focus and team, the plans had been fully executed upon rather than partially fulfilled.

And that's when I realized the final elements of revitalization: Each place needs its own story and dedicated actors to narrate it. The answer to that essential question: *What can only happen here?*

One of the fringe cities on our list was Montgomery, Alabama, a place I knew little about beyond the heroic stories of Dr. Martin Luther King Jr. and the bus boycotts that helped launch the civil rights movement.

I'd read an article about a visionary at work trying to reimagine the city, constructing the shift around an acknowledgment of the victims of lynching there—and a flash point in a larger mission to mark sites of lynchings of African Americans around the country. Bryan Stevenson, a civil rights leader and lawyer, was like a beacon, standing out even among stories of profound change and loss. His work wasn't only about reckoning with this dark history in America; it was about reshaping how we, as a nation, carry that history forward. And, to do so, he needed to build something.

I had no expectations he would respond, but I was compelled to reach out with a straightforward email introducing myself, mentioning the work I'd done, and expressing my admiration. I mentioned a *New York Times* article I had read about his vision for Montgomery, and I expressed how this should take shape as a physical embodiment and memorial. It sat in my email drafts for nearly a month before I got the courage to hit send.

But just days later, to my amazement, I received a reply from Stevenson himself. "We're beginning to think through this now," he wrote. "Would you be willing to come talk with our team?"

I jumped onto a plane as soon as I could. It was April 2015.

Chapter 6

THE MEMORIAL

Montgomery, Alabama

I touched down in Montgomery in the late morning on a Wednesday, stepping off the plane into thick southern air that clung to the skin, summoned here to meet Bryan Stevenson. But the trip felt bigger than any single meeting. In many ways, this city seemed like a chapter from an American story I'd already begun to learn: broken in parts, resilient in others, a place where nostalgia and history obscure the innovative seeds germinating beneath the soil.

Driving through Montgomery, there are countless glimpses of both beauty and neglect. Historic façades, their paint both peeled and overlayered, with windows boarded, stood next to vacant lots. Parking structures of the urban renewal vintage lined the center city. One building had collapsed, with only the brick façade being held up by steel girders. The city felt raw, empty, abandoned, and familiar. It was a signal that battle sites, when hard fought, leave scars in the built world. But for those who know the story, this was no ordinary place. This was where Dr. Martin Luther King Jr. had spoken from church pulpits and led a movement that changed history. It was where Rosa Parks had refused to surrender her seat and where a single decision on a city bus ignited a national fire.

Winding through Montgomery's streets, one feels the presence of both the past and the future. There are reminders everywhere: small brass plaques, crumbling monuments, and street names marking the city's civil rights legacy. And yet, Confederate flags and memorials lingered, holding space for a different version of history. Other banal signs marked insignificant events around the White House of the Confederacy as if those held similar weight to the heroism of the era of civil rights, America's third founding. It was as if two versions of Montgomery coexisted—one pressing forward and another clinging to the past. The contradiction was jarring but also made sense in a place where history was currency and narrative was king.

The steps of the state capitol appeared as if they were rising from the steam in the distance as I looked down Dexter Avenue. The Greek Revival capitol dome punctuated above, lifted up like it was on a dais, floating on smoke. My mind went to the enslaved people who were marched up this street in chains from the riverbanks. The savory smell of soft tar and soil and the moisture of the southern air were faint and foreign in my nostrils.

At the base of Dexter Avenue in Court Square stands a fountain wrapped in iron entanglements, surrounded by cobblestones, all within a roundabout. Beyond this, government buildings. Lining the street outside the government buildings were a half dozen sturdy steel markers. Placed four feet up from the ground, with text explaining the presumptive importance of this place and where it stands in history. Markers were everywhere.

This fountain is a hinge in the city. It connects Dexter, running east–west, and Commerce, running northwest–southeast, which together form the spine of downtown Montgomery. They are short stretches that meet and end at the fountain.

Commerce Street is the name for the city's main commercial strip, connecting the riverbank to the market. Presumably it was named for the commodities that flowed up from the river steamboats gridlocked on the windy riverbanks and the railroad cars that lined them during the nineteenth century. The markers at the fountain and the river tell us that this was Montgomery's commercial heyday, its boom time, its halcyon era. These commodities were then marched up to the intersection of Commerce and Market Street (which is now Dexter) and sold at a fenced-in circular market pit. These commodities, as they were referred to, were enslaved human beings.

Human slaves stood in this pit, and they were marketed, they were assessed, and they were sold into households and plantations throughout the lower southern states. Montgomery was the largest domestic slave–trading post in the United States. Four hundred thousand human beings came through this marketplace—twice the population of Montgomery today. And now a fountain sits where they were sold, spewing water from conches held amid pruned pastoral scenes by gaily frolicking cherubs.

Walking up Dexter Avenue, to where Dr. King set his long crusade in motion, I felt its proximity to power. The capital was just one full block away, and images came to mind of 1965, when King and others had marched from Selma to Montgomery and ended on the grand neoclassical capitol steps, where he looked back down the hill at a sea of people filling the street and recited his speech with its famous refrain, "How long? Not long." He had arrived in Montgomery only eleven years prior, in 1954, and landed at Dexter Avenue Church, foisted into a moment of leadership and outrage he helped steer. He stood on those steps in 1965, on the cusp of the passing of the Voting Rights Act a few months later, his church in his line of sight, and his history for those crucial eleven years of activism flattened in stark relief.

From the vantage point of the steps from where King would have looked out are signs and statues flanking the capitol that mark this place, claiming its historical import.

On either side of King were larger-than-life-size statues.

On King's right, cloaked in his secessionist Confederate costume, was Jefferson Davis, who on these very steps was inaugurated the first and only president of the confederacy in 1861. Montgomery was chosen as the first capital in February of that year, but then moved in May, three months later, to Richmond, closer to the battle lines. And yet, for only three months, Davis's history, his first White House of the Confederacy, and its three-month stint as capitol garner this memorial celebration. None of those details are written in the inscription of the plaque at the base of the statue.

On King's left is a statue of a man in a doctor's coat, Dr. James Marion Sims, with the inscription "Father of Modern Gynecology." Sims conducted surgical experiments to develop techniques in women's health but did so on enslaved women in the 1840s in Montgomery, who lacked autonomy and gave no consent. These experiments happened without anesthesia.

I thought about the meaning of this archetype of design, of the memorials I had come to learn about. Compared to houses, hospitals, or schools, memorials might seem abstract. They don't immediately serve a practical purpose, like providing shelter or subsistence. But they stand as anchors in time, places where we are invited to pause, to confront, to remember. And they are erected amid the public realm, throughout cities and locations marking events and people. What purpose did they serve, and why did people feel compelled to return to them, to build them? What stories were they telling, and which were they hiding between the lines, behind that stone and brass and marble, in plain sight?

Some history is written in textbooks, some is told as myth, some stories are told through cultural practice, and some stories never make it to text at all, but in the built environment, history is written in statues and buildings, in streets, signs, and flags. These are the symbols of the built world, and they tell us stories. Stories of who matters, who held power, who made history, and also, if we look deep enough, whom we try to forget and what we have tried to erase. Our built world is one large, overlapping collage of symbols. And as we walk through it, consciously aware or not, we are being presented with a narrative of place. A story written of our home and of our nation often without seeing who wields the pen.

Each of these is a marker. Formed memorials to history. The sign, the statue, the street name, the fountain, the state house. The flag, while temporal, is only the most visible. But among us, all around us, wherever we walk, it is a palimpsest of symbols and messages, and stories fighting for attention and settling into our purview. I wonder how much King felt this presence of history standing on that staircase in 1965. I began to see it everywhere after that trip. These stories proliferate and compose our built world, much like the very bricks that make up the walls around us.

These thoughts stayed with me as I met Bryan's team at the Equal Justice Initiative's headquarters. There was a quiet intensity among them, the shared commitment to something more profound than individual ambition. Stevenson's vision was to map our nation's unmarked history, to create a physical space for stories that had been left out of the narrative and too often left to fade into silence. This work was not only about the past but about what it means to face the future fully, to acknowledge pain and reckon with memory in order to; step forward. It was a palpable vision unlike any other I had experienced.

He was kind, patient, and fixated on getting to the bigger goal. We sat around the table, with his deputies and colleagues, all lawyers and activists. I learned about the EJI's amazing work across the country, fighting for the imprisoned and the condemned, and from this perch on Commerce Street, they were building a movement on rethinking our moral imagination—and how we should fight for those we cannot fully see, for names we may never recover, for stories we have lost.

But, Bryan said, the work was hindered by our nation's "smog" of racial difference, which makes it hard to see each other in full. To change it, we have to change the stories around us, he said, and build new memorials that counter the big lie of these markers we see that lend permission to believe racial difference is real.

I had compiled a presentation to frame how to think about memorials and what they should do. I pulled out my laptop, fumbled with an HDMI cord, and projected some ideas I'd put together onto their screen to share thoughts on how we could think about memorials as a category.

———

There are four types of memorials, as I understand them: memorials that mark, that provoke, that evoke, and that immerse.

I presented a taxonomy of memorials that had inspired me in order to ask the deeper questions—what is a memorial and what should we expect it to do?

Mark

The most common memorial, those that mark, are all around us. Signs, plaques, inscriptions in the public realm that tell a story and mark place and time. I would put most figurative sculptures into this category, too. Those that resemble a historic figure are like markers themselves, even though they are three-dimensional and figurative and artistic. Their power is in their effort to claim space for past figures and narrate historic events. They can be immeasurably valuable, but they can also fade into the background, ignored by the public as a remnant of the past.

In Montgomery, there were signs of this everywhere. Like Boston, where I was living at the time, Montgomery was a city obsessed with the nostalgia for what was once here. A story of former greatness—but, as Bryan made evident, the stories were often inaccurate, usually incomplete, and sometimes banal and strange. One sign in Montgomery was about a tea party held in the home of an antebellum city elite. Another that recognized Rosa Parks had the country music legend Hank Williams recognized on its back. It read like an act of dilution, intentional or not, though I safely presumed the former. To equate the world-changing work of Rosa Parks with a musical star had the effect to make her appear small, to introduce false equivalence, to let the story fade into irrelevance.

Bryan's team was already changing this work and commissioning historical markers for sites of real import, and for locations of immense pain and violence. These were powerful corrections that would be meaningful, emotional, and potentially provoking.

Provoke

The most well-known memorial that provokes a reaction is the Vietnam Veterans Memorial in Washington, DC, by Maya Lin, built in 1982.

"My father," I told Bryan's team as I continued my presentation, "took me whenever he could to see the memorials in DC." We'd lived in Maryland for three years of my childhood, moving there when I was eight years old so my father could test out his political ambitions. He was often homesick, so his friends from the Hudson Valley would visit us on many weekends and we'd take them around Washington to see the memorials and museums. The Vietnam Veterans Memorial left an impression I'd never forget.

I admit, at first I hated it. I was eight. What didn't I hate? At first glance, and without historical context, it was a mass of names on a wall that felt repetitive and simple. But over time, I would understand how complex it really was. Visiting as an adult, I walked along the path that descends slowly at a slight angle (a "scar" in the earth Lin called it), and the wall on my left side rose to be taller than my body, much taller, like I was descending below the earth. And then the polished granite of the wall with its etched names struck me. It was so reflective any visitor would see themselves in it. It was like a mirror in stone. But the names of the fifty-eight thousand dead or gone missing in action listed one after the other in the reflection made the visitor more than a witness—I could have been one of them.

Visitors around the memorial were searching, actively engaged, and looking for the name of their family or friends, like a massive puzzle. And when they found it, they would stop and touch the name, following the etched line in the granite with their finger. And then some would pull out pencil and paper and scratch the graphite sideways on the paper over the name to create a rubbing, leaving a negative white gap of the letters in its etched font, the result surrounded by a loose angled scratching of gray.

That paper would depart the site with them, a remnant of their visit, proof they had come to witness and to take home something with them to remember.

This was the provocation. Markers and statues encouraged the visitor to learn and reflect, but it was generally a passive experience that one could opt into or out of. Provoking, instead, encouraged action from the visitor to search, to touch, to document, and then to bring something away with them, a remnant they could call their own. It was engaging the body in a haptic, tactile way, instead of only in a more passive way, what we see and read. The tactile memory is different from the interpretive memory, taking in the experience through our bodies as well as our minds.

Maya Lin, the artist, who was a student at Yale when she submitted the Vietnam memorial proposal, caused a national controversy with her win. Ornate, faceted, neoclassical memorials to Jefferson and Lincoln lined the mall. They were constructed of white marble, had statues, and were made by the great architects of the era. The Vietnam memorial design was too simple and minimalist and "abstract," as some called it. Where were the figures of the soldiers and the statues? Where was the explanatory text? And who was this student, with no experience, creating a national symbol of loss for our war?

The controversy stirred so much resistance that a second memorial infamously was commissioned at the entrance to the memorial. Created by Frederick Hart, it consists of three soldiers, in their army gear, weapons over shoulders, looking out at the horizon—a stark figure to contrast the abstract scar it overlooks.

Lin's Vietnam memorial has stood the test of time, however. It has become recognized as one of the watershed moments in monument making and public memory because its simple ingredients asked for more. They gave just enough to allow the visitor to invest themselves in the act of memorialization as well and to find their own paths toward recognition.

It is also now one of the only things I remember from my time as a kid in Washington. It is seared into my brain just as it's seared into the brains of so many others. That is provocation.

Evoke

There is a third type of memorial that is neither physical nor sculptural but ephemeral and bound with time. It communicates the intangible. These are memorials that can be events, or shows of light or sound installation, and be experiences that happen through interaction and ritual.

I moved next to a slide of the 9/11 memorial, designed by Michael Arad, whose giant cavernous pits show the volume of absence, presenting depths too deep to see below, and thereby suggesting infinity and a removal of what was there. But the full evocation happens on the renewal date of September 11, when giant spotlights beam up from near where the towers stood, creating a light shaft that can be seen from the entire city and far beyond. This light installation shows what once was without reconstructing it.

All sorts of memorializing actions are evocations of memories and actions communities seek to recover. But memorials that evoke are about utilizing more abstract design elements to trigger sensory responses. Through light, through sound, through smell or touch, these experiences are designed so that they must be experienced firsthand to fully absorb them. And often those experiences are projected through rituals—repeated, time-stamped events.

I told the Stevenson group of my work in Rwanda, how some friends and colleagues I'd gathered were survivors themselves of the genocide. Every single one had family either killed or involved in the killing. The gravity of their truth telling and healing had been instructive of what is possible.

Rwanda had been building memorials throughout this dark period in history, and in 2004 completed a national genocide memorial, ten years after the genocide and three years before I arrived. It was already a significant international destination.

At the museum, an open grave drew visitors from around the country each first week of April to take part in a mass remembrance. Those who had discovered remains of bodies in their land or in their districts would bring those remains, unidentified, and inter them together in the unfinished space.

People wept as they prayed and acknowledged the lives lost in a country now reborn and rebuilt.

I told Bryan about the bringing and taking away of this memorial, the ritual and spectacle and grief, had been overwhelming as it provided room for healing as well. Its power was immense.

In Rwanda, this "memorial week" was broadcast across the country. On national television, it was a public and shared act of exhaustive, painful release, exposed for all to witness.

Evocation is spiritual and sensory. It suggests that not all memorials are physical and that some are celebratory, commemorative rituals of participation and action. Without the actions of the present, the memorializing actions would cease to exist.

Immerse

Memorials that immerse take time to walk through and engage oneself fully into, and they require more space, more environment, more landscape. It is a total environment, a place one is meant to emerge different after going through it. These memorials are meant to provide a transcendent experience.

I think of the pilgrimage journeys to Mecca or the Vatican City, or the long multi-day journeys on the Camino de Santiago in Spain, or the Inca Trail that ends at Machu Picchu in Peru. In discussions with Bryan's team, I talked about Montgomery as a location like this, the end of the five-day trek from Selma for Dr. King and his supporters from March 21 to 25, 1965.

Immersion calls for a total sensory experience that creates a sense of solemnity and repose. It also asks you where you are. A great cathedral has a different sound environment than an outdoor space. Moisture and the sound of water can be relaxing, as Dr. Farmer taught me in Rwanda with his insistence on building koi ponds. But there are other senses that space heightens. As Susan Magsamen and Ivy Ross explain in their book *Your Brain on Art*, there is also our vestibular sense, which helps us maintain stability and drives our movement. It is controlled by the fluid in our inner ear. And then there is the proprioceptive sense, or the kinesthetic sense, which is our body's ability to know our locations in space without relying on sight. These senses allow us to know where we are standing and where our limbs are in space to help us stand upright, duck our head walking under a low doorjamb, or get to level ground as we exit a ramp. Do you ever notice how you want to keep moving on a ramp and not stand still? This is the vestibular and proprioceptive senses operating.

––––––

Architecture and design make use of these phenomena all the time. We study and employ the ways in which the built world around us can coerce us to move, to feel, and to perceive. The visual vertical sense is another example, as neuroscientist Andrew Huberman explains, that combines these vestibular, proprioceptive, and visual senses to result in our inclination as humans to orient our heads and bodies in a position that allows us to view the whole environment, and creates a desire to keep the horizon in front of us level and a view of the landscape present. We naturally gravitate toward that expansive view, where cues taken from the available data help us gain orientation and spatial awareness. Some researchers suggest that seeing the horizon is rooted in evolution, in the early hominid brain to survey safety and opportunity. I'm no anthropologist, but that does makes sense in my experience. When there is a tower, I want to climb it and get to the top and look out. When there is a vista, I want to survey the land and know where I am. We share this hunger for "the horizon."

The Memorial to the Murdered Jews of Europe in Berlin is one of the more notable examples of immersive memorialization in the modern day. I had visited the piece, completed in 2005 and designed by the architect Peter Eisenman with early support from the artist Richard Serra, shortly before the EJI meeting. The experience came with me as I grasped pieces of its pilgrimage aesthetic qualities home after taking in the work. Eisenman's memorial is a landscape of grave-like boxes, extruded from the ground, with no visible entrance or exit. As a result it "appears" on the edge of four roads, with freeform entry points selected by those who venture into the space. In my experience the vista evoked a cemetery, that ancient landscape experience when people arrive to commune with our dead. But there are no plantings here, no grave markers in granite standing upright and proud from the ground. No, this landscape utilizes stone and gravel beneath the natural setting of those who come to remember.

And then the ground slopes in different directions, inevitably drawing the visitor down into a maze that is at once disorienting and unsettling. The horizon or vertical visual sense is lost suddenly, and the grave-like stones (which he calls *stelae,* upright stone slabs or pillars typically used as monuments or markers) loom overhead and create a labyrinthine, tunnel-like environment where corners and ends become nothingness.

Architects have always wrestled with maze-like environments. Whether shaped by intention, constraint or circumstance, the labyrinth leaves us unmoored, testing our proprioceptive and vestibular senses. In this disoriented state, when we feel lost, we must rely on sight, sound, and touch to help reorient and find our way. In Berlin, of course, this is intentional, but there are times when structures made necessary by engineering, safety, or other outside concerns interfere with the flow of space and dislocate the humans interacting with a built environment.

In Berlin, when the ground slopes up and down, this disorientation comes to the fore. I experienced it myself as I traversed the memorial's terrain and found myself "lost" within it. At some point, as I walked in search of a door, arrow, or other orienting artifact, I instead was confronted with a staircase leading downward and into the ground. It was the entrance to the museum of the Holocaust, placed unexpectedly. I walked down and soon found myself underneath the stelae, seeing now how they filtered light from above, supported in their task by structures etched with the names and stories of the dead, situated so their data would be projected into the depths of the memorial and made one with the surroundings.

This memorial had no hierarchy of entrance, no signage instructing people where they stood or were expected to go next. Because of this, the edges of the space were porous, and while some, like myself, were there for an immersive solemn experience, others, children and young people, ran around as if it were a playground, jumping onto the boxes, delighting in the stelae and interplay of shadow and light, playing hide-and-seek. The effect was not without controversy, and

I shared that with Stevenson as I made the case to retain some level of that freedom in a new design.

Some people loved that the architecture allowed visitors to find their own way—the way it prioritized discovery and an internal experience through heightened senses rather than demanding a certain response aligned with the memorial's preferences. While this lack of hierarchy did lend itself to people using the memorial as something perhaps unintended, the alternative would be imperfect as well. A prescribed experience is, in its way, an authoritarian experience.

A sign narrates a history authored by a perspective. A statue selects heroic characters to author a story of hagiographic lineage. Both signal what the public should acknowledge and what it should not. But then, what is lost when ambiguity is ruled out of the equation? How can any single narrator claim to capture the full breadth of an historical event or era? And even within the customary range of storytelling, who decides which slivers of that story come first and take precedence? This all seemed ripe for exploration.

———

I became interested in memorials, I told the Stevenson group, when I studied in South Africa during college and lived in Capetown afterward, before my father got sick. There, in the aftermath of Apartheid, memorials and museums were prominently deployed to heal the nation with the aspiration they would lead the country through the wilderness and into something better.

Johannesburg's Apartheid Museum makes evident the stakes of what you are stepping into. Tickets give entrance to one of two racially categorized gates—one for "non-white" (encapsulating those who are "native," "coloured," or "Asian," in South Africa's official parlance) and one for "white." The ticket one receives is random, but once assigned, the entrance is firm: One cannot enter the "coloured" or "white" gate without the corresponding ticket.

This entrance experience, unlike the Holocaust memorial, is didactic and provocative. It feels uncomfortable to be forced to enter one door or another, and thus the museum, operating spatially, presents a microcosm of that racist, white supremacist history and forces all to experience that humiliation and division firsthand, whether they would have been subjected to its punishments or not.

When you are inside, the museum shows the reality of differentiated experience and access. The ticket determines which version of the museum one is allowed to access, not just the door entered. There is a sense of loss generated by the knowledge that your neighbor in line to enter will see items and learn stories you will not, all due to an arbitrary decision made by a force beyond your grasp.

And it was a reminder of the power of a building. The space around us was determinative in so many ways. By imposing discomfort, anxiety, disorientation, release, and revelation, racist regimes knew, and know, the power of a building.

———

Germany, South Africa, and Rwanda had committed to the construction of memorials intended to heal the defects of their nations, but the US had never done this before. Bryan reminded us of a key portion of our task, to understand the reasons so much had been invested in memorials and markers dedicated to holding up and preserving our own racist traditions and commitments to racial difference.

———

Germany is a country that has historically embraced a full accounting with its past, and I nearly came face-to-face with this fact. I was walking around the streets of Berlin one evening in 2012. It was cold and rainy, and I was looking for a place to stay warm. As I huddled for protection from the elements, I gazed down and nearly slipped on the smooth surface of one of the cobblestones that make up many of the sidewalks and plazas of the city. But this one had been slicked brass, with letters on it. I read the inscription, which shared the name of someone murdered in the Holocaust and their last known shelter before being taken.

The Stolpersteine ("stumbling stones") commenced installation in 1995, initiated by German artist Gunter Demnig. The project started with a couple dozen unauthorized stones placed in Cologne as an art installation, but it grew as Demnig sought to commemorate individual victims of the Holocaust—Jews, Roma, disabled individuals, and others persecuted by the Nazi regime.

It was only after a few years that the first legally approved Stolpersteine were laid in Austria; legal recognition followed in Germany, and the Stolpersteine have since spread throughout Europe. Each Stolpersteine is a small brass-plated stone embedded in the sidewalk in front of the last known residence of a Holocaust victim. By now, over 107,000 Stolpersteine have been placed across Europe, making it one of the largest decentralized memorial projects in the world.

After Berlin, I came to this realization: Great memorials must achieve two things at once. A great memorial must tell the individual story—the *intimate* story of the one individual we can name and see ourselves in their story, asking the question: Could that have been me? And a great memorial must tell the *infinite* story—the large, uncountable, immeasurable whole of an atrocity, event, or system that is impossible to fully grasp. The Stolpersteine captured in a distributed way both the intimate and the infinite. Bryan wanted to place markers with a similar spirit to these at the sites of lynchings across the American South. I was here to participate in that vision.

Bryan was not sure if it should be a single statue in a patch of green behind the office or something bigger, but he wanted to commemorate first the 364 recorded victims of lynching in the state of Alabama. His eventual goal would grow to ten more memorials, one for every capital city of the former confederate states.

He asked me to think about ideas of how to build a memorial to the lynching victims here and eventually spread throughout the country.

———

I left Montgomery energized. Bryan's team had a sober power and righteousness I felt seduced by. It felt like you were on the right team when among them. Bryan was generous and kind and had a calm power and surefootedness I could not help but hope to impress.

This was a huge opportunity I could not pass up. There was no commission, no business pitch, no contract. I simply made contact and was given license to test ideas.

When I had a moment to think through the project, I was struck by the unknowability of the future memorials. If there was one now and ten more later, then this first initiative needed to have replicable DNA. It needed to have a form that could be redeployed at a future time, to some future site that we could not now determine. It needed something simple, like the Stolpersteine.

The memorial should be a pilgrimage site for people to journey to but also provide something visitors could take home with them, like at the Vietnam Veterans War Memorial. Having an action, a sense of urgency, would provide the possibility of movement. Regrettably I'd felt a sense of paralysis after leaving Rwanda's genocide memorial.

It was painful and meant to be painful. But the action—what we can do—in that new awakened space was not clear. I felt bludgeoned and hopeless. Bryan wanted the opposite. He sought to tell difficult truths but to be left with hope in the end.

———

I wanted to give tools to those who could bring something home with them.

It is rare that a first sketch after hours becomes the final product, but the seed of the design came to me in my sketchbook that summer, during a festival in June 2015.

The sketch showed a marker, the size of a column or a coffin, suspended above a person, and a roof of these suspended columns. This was intended to evoke the hangings—lynchings—this memorial sought to memorialize. Then a character walking through that field witnessing the markers above and below from a hill in the middle. Some markers would be suspended, and others could be configured in different ways depending on the site.

I developed the plan further. There would need to be 364 markers, in different configurations, one for each victim, and I wanted to make these markers out of concrete, mixed with the soil from the sites of lynching where those victims were killed. For the ten other memorials, this simple marker-and-soil combination would allow us many other configurations, but ultimately, after testing a few different versions, four thousand or so would have to be built.

Bryan gave me the charge to be creative, and while the markers were to my mind inspired, there was further to go. Ideas of different size and stature for him to consider.

The first idea was a statue, configured of one marker commemorating the Alabama victims of lynching, suspended on a contraption in a patch of grass near his office on Montgomery's Coosa Street. This memorial could be sculptural and carry some text of significance as it held a spot in the city.

The next, larger version was a memorial of 364 markers, all in a field or forest where a visitor would walk among them. Each marker being both the same visually but also dedicated and unique to a single victim. It would be an evocative memorial that also marked. Something that suggested absence and potential of ten more to be built at a future date.

Last, I offered a third vision. A national memorial in Montgomery that would forego the ten other memorials that were indeterminate—this would fully grasp the narrative scope of Bryan's vision. Funding for the ten more was uncertain, as was the ability to obtain land at scale, and the potential addition of many complicated political processes to build ten statewide memorials. And there would also be a double marker. One that was in Montgomery and one that was to be claimed by someone else to take with them back to their home.

This would be an immersive experience that required more land (six acres) and more money, but we'd only need to do it once. The overall price would be much lower, but we would need a much larger initiative to build from the start. This would be an experiential pilgrimage site.

I suggested we could still use the markers, but we would count them as representative of counties instead of individuals. Each stricken county would be represented by a marker bearing the names of the people who had been lynched there. This would give us a total of around eight hundred markers we'd have to construct. Each marker would tie us intimately to a place—but collected together would feel overwhelming and infinite. Built in a "frame," a way to account for the unaccountable and hold space for the erased.

I showed the team a design that walked them through different stages of transformation. Bryan wanted it to be very directed and not allow space for children or others to misinterpret the somberness of this sacred site. The memorial, he said, should be a pathway through a series of stages of transformation.

Reading Bryan's work and his book *Just Mercy*, I noted his criteria for overcoming the fog of racial difference. He mentioned four stages, and I found a fifth he alluded to. Those five were: 1. Identity matters; 2. Get uncomfortable; 3. Get proximate; 4. Change narrative; and 5. Remain hopeful; against all odds. I showed how the visitor could experience each of these stages as they walked into the memorial.

"Identity"—the first stage—would be represented by simply inscribing the name of the victim—their birth and death and county—onto the marker. Then we could arrange those markers into a field of markers and counties naming the more than four thousand victims Bryan and his team had counted.

Discomfort could be achieved by having the ground ramp down as the markers suddenly rose above you, revealing the unstable ground and the proprioceptive feeling of your body with these markers rising above you while you descend. This would be an eerie and disconcerting moment. The markers, once they rise above your head, would make you feel like you are under the earth, and also underneath the representative "body" the marker stood for.

Third would be narrative change, and Bryan suggested statements on the wall communicating the banality of these stories. The ground would descend as more and more of the markers collected in the final corner. Here, the words would be harder to read and county markings left illegible. This would share that infinite condition where information is just out of reach.

At this corner of markers, which I called the chapel space, there would be a water wall and seating for visitors to reflect. The sound of the water and tactile sensation of moisture and humidity would expand the perception of what this hallowed space represented. Cleansing us. This was the fourth stage, proximity, a theory of Bryan's about finding commonality and intelligence from the people and places we visit.

Bryan showed me photographs of lynchings, one of which, of Henry Smith in Paris, Texas, in 1893, remains ingrained in my mind as it overwhelms with its brutality and public acceptance. In the image Bryan shared, Mr. Smith is brought to a wooden dais purpose-built for this act, as a crowd looks on. The spectacle was the point, as Bryan would articulate. Exposing children and women to the possibility of murder carried out with permission and in public. I thought of the unseen someone who'd built this dais, and what Mr. Smith observed overlooking the crowd. I wanted to replicate that experience but invert it, with the memorial judging you, the visitor, as you stood silently on a platform placed in the center of the hill after snaking through the markers. The visual vertical sense activated now, looking out over everything, is a moment of empowerment, like the dead are in judgment of the living, and asking you, the visitor, what you will do to resist this behavior in the future.

I offered a final condition upon descent. Visitors would see a field of duplicate memorial markers, the same as the ones suspended above us but now lying in the field in rows alphabetically. The offending counties across the United States would be encouraged to claim their marker, once the right conditions were met, and bring it home with them to place on their own land. This would not only achieve the distributed effect of the Stolpersteine but also give visitors a tool to enact remembrance where it mattered, in their home county, in their community, where these vicious crimes were allowed to happen and persist for far too long.

This was participation. The final act. The memorial was

vulnerable and would change over time. It would only be complete once the public took responsibility and participated in it. Only when all the markers in the field had been collected and this brutal chapter of history accepted would it be "complete."

———

In walking around Montgomery, I learned of First Baptist Church, otherwise known as the Brick-a-Day church, where Ralph Abernathy, MLK's deputy and close confidant, was pastor. This was the site of the siege of May 21, 1961, when Freedom Riders who were met with violence at the Greyhound station in Montgomery were then besieged by a few thousand whites who threatened to burn the church down. The governor had, at the urging of Robert Kennedy, ordered the National Guard to protect First Baptist and end the mob violence. Like so many parts of Montgomery, this site held powerful standing in our nation's reconstruction.

I was fascinated by its name. It was first erected in 1867 as one of the earliest Black churches in the city, and it got its name after it was rebuilt in 1915 following a fire; each congregant brought a "brick a day" to rebuild it. Hence its name. I loved this idea that we bring the soil and bricks to build the things we need and love. What if, instead of bringing soil from the sites to pour into the markers or make into bricks, we could collect soil in jars, asking people to participate as we gathered raw materials for the site of the memorial? We could display these jars and organize them into a simple installation that would speak to the power of a community coming together to take part and remember and say the names of those who'd been lost to hatred.

Bryan's organization immediately went for this idea. They had already initiated a community remembrance project, where people would find and research names of these victims. Now they could collect soil and bring it to the center, and we could display it. Our team designed a simple shelving system for the EJI's headquarters, and using plain glass jars we organized the display.

EJI housed the jars in their conference room at first, and walking in, after the jars began to accumulate, it smelled of earth, and the wall, with dozens of different tones of soil, revealed the simple and obvious truth: that no two soil colors are exactly the same and that there is infinite variation.

The experience collecting soil made me change the noted design of the markers. Instead of cast concrete—heavy and foreboding—we suggested changing to a Corten steel, known as weathering steel, because while it begins almost silver, it quickly oxidizes and changes into hues of purple then brown, then orange and pockets of amber. No two would be the same, and they change when moisture and rain weather them. The markers evolve and change and then drip a rust-colored water on the wall, staining and coloring it. I said it was as if these markers would be living, bleeding, and changing the place around us. Bryan agreed.

The EJI team went on a hunt to find a home. We looked at two sites in Montgomery that could hold six acres and one, only a few blocks from EJI's office, sat on a hill overlooking the city. It was the second-tallest hill in Montgomery, next to the capitol, but the property around it was devastated. There were old mansions where entire walls had fallen down and trees had risen up through them. Other properties were vacant except for staircases that had once been, but were no longer, attached to the front porches of old houses. These were made of brick and left behind a ghost neighborhood, a place where lives were once lived and nothing remained. Montgomery was not in good shape.

The site was grand and vivid. Bryan and I walked to the top, looking out over the city, and pointed to everything we could see if we built there. The choice was obvious, but the task would not be simple. There were twenty-six other landowners we'd need to assemble and replant, combining the plots to create a bigger six-acre parcel.

"Yes, but we'd have the second hill," I said. "You should buy all the land around here, Bryan. This memorial will change this city."

He agreed, but his true vision was grander, far bigger than I could see.

———

When the Montgomery memorial opened in 2018, over fifty thousand people attended the opening. Bryan and his team had raised millions of dollars and manifested this vision into something otherworldly. Folks from around the country and world came to see it and be part of it. During the years of construction, a lot of naysayers told us no one would come to Montgomery, but thousands did, and then millions more followed as the years wore on.

At the opening, I was with friends and staff. My mother, my wife, and my in-laws were there. Paul Farmer was also there and even friends from Poughkeepsie. I had been invited to a morning meeting by one of the funders of the memorial to speak. There, I met two amazing ladies who came up to me after I explained the memorial and how it was designed.

Pamela Bosley and Annette Nance-Holt introduced themselves to me at a pre-opening event organized by a memorial funder that auspicious morning. They handed me a business card with their names, and on the back side were images of their children, Terrell Bosley and Blair Holt. Their boys had been killed by random gun violence in Chicago, they told me, and their organization, Purpose

Over Pain, needed my help. "We need a memorial to our children dying in this epidemic," Pam said to me, hands holding mine. I had trouble holding back tears as they shared their stories.

The torrent of emotions continued in these earliest days of our work in Montgomery. To see the project manifested in real time, full of people admiring it and experiencing the immersion, was overwhelming to me. I tried to gather myself in the chapel space and felt the moisture of the water wall touch my skin. My friend Hank Willis Thomas, an artist whose sculpture, *Raise Up*, was integrated into the memorial in Alabama, walked around the corner and moved next to me as I sat.

I told him about my conversation with Pam and Annette. Hank's cousin and best friend, Songha, had also been killed by guns. He told me he had been murdered in Philadelphia, just for wearing a chain and being in the wrong place. Thomas said this was an opportunity to do something that was necessary. He wanted to do it together.

I searched my memory for inspiration, an idea that could stand up to this awesome task of remembrance for so many current victims and so many who were young. When I was living in South Africa, one of the more powerful exhibits I had ever seen was a show in the prison cells of Robben Island. The exhibit showcased personal mementos, letters, photos, and items that former prisoners and visitors had donated back to the prison. Visitors typically saw only the cell Nelson Mandela was once held in, which usually had a rolled-up blanket and small table in the room. The other rooms were empty. However, each cell was adorned with a single item. One cell had a picture of a loved one, another cell a meaningful poem pinned to the wall. One cell had a saxophone that was made out of tin soup cans. A political prisoner named Dikobe Ben Martins fashioned it out of scrap materials in the prison.

I looked down the cell block and there were dozens more rooms, and I had only a few minutes more to see the exhibit before the tour moved on. I'd had this small window into the lives of a few prisoners and their acts of resistance and survival, but there were so many more.

To me, that shared something crucial with the epidemic of gun violence. Seven hundred people a week killed. I asked Hank, "What if we could have victims' families bring objects and we collect them and store them in these houses, glass houses, where there is space for objects to be shown and revealed?" Like in South Africa. One object per person that they curate. And too many to count.

We could have the houses be in each state Hank mentioned. And we could do a national memorial to gun violence that would collect objects for years. My colleague Jha D Amazi and I aspired to place it one day on the National Mall, weaving into the lineage of protests like Resurrection City built during the Poor People's Campaign in 1968, or Cleve Jones's AIDS Quilt from 1987.

Our next project, the National Memorial to Victims of Gun Violence, emerged as I sat there imagining what other problems we could think through in art and activism.

———

I began to see the built world as one big litany of legends and stories fighting to be told. This fight, to speak truth in the built world, to peel back its façade, takes political might. And it showed the daily amnesia we wield to cope with and suffer through the symbolic barrage of markers, reminders, and testimonies of who scripts our past.

This is what a memorial can do. This is why we engrave words, etch steel, and carve marble to remember. These memorials force confrontation and fill space—physical and psychological—

otherwise open to the perpetrators those memorials may seek to unmoor. These memorials recall our past, to remind us of who we are today so that we can choose who we want to be tomorrow.

Memorials cannot be neutral. They can either injure or empower. They are doused in our collective memory and set aflame when revisionist histories are allowed to stand.

———

Bryan walked press and media through the Montgomery memorial. He pointed out the name of Reverend T. A. Allen, a minister who he said had been advocating for sharecropper rights. He said, "A lot of these folks were lynched because they showed too much dignity, they showed too much humanity. He just wanted to be respected as a human being, and it got him hanged." Allen was lynched in Mississippi in 1935.

Dignity, that word again. I recalled Paul Farmer claiming to build something with beauty in mind was to dignify it, and by that he meant to make people feel welcome and cared for and their humanity recognized and served. Here, Bryan was mentioning it, too, that the search for dignity, the fight for it, could be activated by the construction of this memorial. It was a through line to dignity construction.

A friend and founding president and CEO of the Eames Institute of Infinite Curiosity, John Cary, had summarized it well. When asked what the impact of design is, he said it is dignity full stop. "Dignity is to design what justice is to law and health is to medicine." He meant that a better-designed world can invigorate the soul and make us feel that we, too, despite all the forces around us, matter.

I wondered if dignity was simply nice to have or rather more elemental, a right we required to thrive. I asked these questions during a talk I had been invited to give by TED, the nonprofit media organization—the same place I'd seen Bryan speak in person for the first time. Afterward, in the hallway of the theater, a person stopped me and introduced himself. His name was Andreas Görgen, and he was director-general for culture and communication at Germany's Federal Foreign Office. He had played a crucial role in initiatives of remembrance and memorialization to the Holocaust.

———

He said to me that it took Germany almost fifty years to commit to memorialization and confront the horrors of the holocaust and World War II. He said that two generations were probably needed to fully embrace the past, and he mentioned a key component that facilitated the embrace.

West Germany's new constitution, written after World War II, but well before reunification, enshrined the right to human dignity into law. "Human dignity shall be inviolable. To respect and protect it shall be the duty of all state authority." The emphasis on human dignity was a response to the atrocities of the Nazi era, and after reunification in 1990, West and East Germany adopted what was called the Basic Law, the *Grundgesetz*. This led to all sorts of reforms in Germany, from housing to public space to memorials, but also to reforming prisons, shifting them from a punitive model to a rehabilitative model over punishment.

Bryan's work was mostly around the incarcerated, and I wondered, if we could make architecture foster healing and advance dignity, what about the architecture that extracts dignity, that hurts and oppresses people, like prisons? If we are fighting for dignity, shouldn't we also look directly at the infrastructure that is actively reducing dignity in the world?

The prison seemed to be the most obvious example of where architecture injures.

I opened my email that spring, and in my inbox was a note from a friend of John Cary's named Sarah Lustbader who was working at the Vera Institute of Justice, trying to reform jails and prisons nationally. She asked if I would join her team to visit these German prisons with an entourage and also go to Norway to see Halden, the most radical prison in the world. I immediately said yes.

When Dr. King spoke at the Oberlin College commencement in 1955, he said, "All mankind is tied together; all life is interrelated, and we are all caught in an inescapable network of mutuality, tied in a single garment of destiny . . . This is the interrelated structure of reality."

The garment of destiny. It is a physical thing, where whatever affects one affects all. The prison, that hidden and buried infrastructure, was the upside-down world of the system we lived in every day, a lens through which we could evaluate our society's commitment to dignity and to justice.

A few weeks after the opening in 2018 in Montgomery of what was ultimately called the National Memorial for Peace and Justice, I found myself in to see the worst that architecture could do and a heroic effort to reform it.

Chapter 7

THE PRISON

Halden, Norway

The complex sat far beyond Oslo's outskirts, past towering fjords and glistening inlets. Occasionally, the surrounding waters caught the light, scattering reflections across the early morning sky, low, orange beams breaking through here and there, momentarily blinding peaks of bright, sharp contrast in the subdued northern landscape. In the distance lay a thin, quiet horizon line stretching out over the vast unknown.

This was Halden Prison, Norway's radical experiment in humane incarceration that at once embodied the promise of a new way forward. Yet it remained, undeniably, a prison: a place of confinement, control, surveillance, and—despite its lofty ideals—suffering.

I was with a group of other curious guests invited by the Vera Institute of Justice. Prison reformers, American correctional officers, policymakers, and even a filmmaker all came together to explore how we might open minds to new models of rehabilitation. Vera had begun a project, Reimagining the Prison in the US, and had asked me to join their tour to investigate the architectural dimensions of reform and speak on the history of prisons. Arriving at Halden, I realized how much more I still had to learn when compared to my fellow travelers.

Halden, our host, was in many ways the most famous prison in the world. Conceptualized in 2007 and inspired by a Norwegian government white paper on punishment titled "Punishment that Works—Less Crime—A Safer Society." Halden represented a wholesale response to shortcomings seen in prison systems worldwide: overemphasis on control, pervasive violence, and stagnant, substandard conditions.

Norwegian reformers and politicians concluded that nothing would truly improve without putting an improved model into practice, and so, they imagined, designed, and built "the world's most humane" prison, Halden, an experiment in treating people with a level of humanity and care typically denied those being held within confinement.

Halden Prison first appears to be what you'd expect of a maximum-security facility—a towering, gray concrete wall, formidable and imposing. The wall stretches high above us, smooth as stone, but there's no barbed wire curling along the top. Instead, there's a curious rounded lip that juts out toward us, sleek and unyielding. At its base, a massive steel door looms, fortified with locks, bolts, and electronic eyes. The concrete block is surrounded by a quiet asphalt lot, ringed with parked cars. It's the first checkpoint, a transition space separating our everyday world from what lies beyond.

The prison's governor, Are Høidal, met the visiting group in that parking lot and gave us a brief introduction, his tone factual, even cordial. At the close he gestured to the entrance, and it was not the grand fortress door that swung open, but a small human-sized door set within it. Behind it, as if passing through a secret threshold, was an entirely unexpected world.

Instead of the bleak asphalt yards Americans have come to expect in a prison, we were greeted by a serene grove of trees and a winding path leading in two directions. To the right stood a small cabin, modest and modern, built of metal panels and wood with large picture windows that gaze out onto the forest. It looked more like a retreat center than a facility for incarcerated men—a design straight out of a Scandinavian design magazine.

Inside, the space only grew more surprising. The cabin opened into a bright, airy room with white walls and cathedral ceilings. A sleek open kitchen greeted us, scattered with everyday culinary items, including an ordinary set of knives in a wooden block. The US correctional officer in the group picked one up, holding it with a look of utter disbelief. "Loose knives . . . in a prison?" he muttered, half in awe, half in horror. "Unthinkable." He was expressing a familiar sentiment: "That's fine for Norway, but it would never work in the United States."

The purpose of this trip was clearly to convince us otherwise.

In the plush sitting area, the low-slung Danish-style furniture—warm wood and soft fabrics in muted tones—faces a wall of glass that opens onto a patio. Outside, there's even a grill. On a low shelf by the couch, wooden toys and puzzles rest in cubbyholes, tidy and inviting.

"This cabin is for family visits," our host told us, room for residents' families, including their children, to stay over for the weekend. With the amenities provided, residents and their visitors are able to prepare meals together, share conversations over dinner, and spend uninterrupted time in a private, comforting home. The idea is to simulate a normal family life, as closely as possible within a prison context. Someone in our group chuckled in disbelief. "In the US, a conjugal visit might mean a mattress in a windowless room." Here, the area was not only spacious and well designed but also deeply intentional in its aspirational ordinariness.

Høidal explained the theory behind the design. "The principle of normality—the idea that life inside prison should be as close as possible to life in the community—is one of the cornerstones of the modern Norwegian correctional system." Residents should maintain their family bonds, experience the routine of life on the outside—even if only for a few days. They cook meals, care for their children, interact as they would in their own homes. It's intended, too, for the children. Instead of forcing them through layers of locked gates, metal detectors, and security checks, children enter this normalized home environment. And instead of the often traumatic experience of intake, children are with their parents in a setting that feels safe and familiar.

The question about the knives arose again, skepticism still lingering in the room. The prison has been developed from the ground up to make everyday life more or less "ordinary." In most prisons, inmates lose the simple skills of managing a household, of making choices. "Here," Høidal explained, "we help them retain those." The designers' vision was that the prison "meets the inmates and employees in a friendly and nonauthoritarian way."

Here, in the heart of a forest enclosed by those towering walls, was a domestic haven, complete with all the markers of home— furniture that invited comfort, toys that spoke to the innocence of children, and the simple, powerful act of sharing a meal. It was designed to be ordinary, but its result to us as guests jolted assumptions and disrupted our deeply ingrained assumptions about what is possible in carceral spaces.

It was a shocking revelation to see, but also much more than just a statement or an image. It exposed a core assumption that shapes the US prison system: that prison must be a place as far removed from home as possible, a place of deprivation and isolation, separate from the idea of family or human dignity.

In Halden, this construct is flipped, challenged by a different approach. Here, it was not about stripping away the comforts and rhythms of life but about making them possible in a controlled, respectful way. The prison aimed not at crushing the spirit but "at returning the inmate home" and to encourage them to reimagine their place within it, and to practice the necessary skills of resocialization. Halden had laid bare a profound truth: the power of architecture and environment to shape lives, even those held within walls.

Someone asked, "What about these trees? What if people climb them?"

"If you climb up the tree, you have to eventually come down," Høidal said calmly, as if it was the most normal answer. Which it was.

What, then, is "normal" about any prison? The prison I had pictured in my mind was constructed from fragments of movies and stories—a stark world of barred cells, where people were enclosed, confined, locked into place. I imagined bodies, stripped of agency, immobilized in cages, robbed of movement, interaction, and action. But as I questioned that preconception, I wondered: Is this confinement meant to mold the incarcerated, to shape them in some deliberate way? Or is it designed only to protect society from the people within?

Are Høidal understood the tension between these questions. After thirty years working as a correctional officer, primarily within Norway's prison system, he had witnessed the evolution of incarceration firsthand. Before leading Halden Prison, Høidal served at Oslo Central Prison, one of the oldest and most traditional in the country. It was a relic of a bygone era—one marked by a very different philosophy of imprisonment, a legacy from the days of Bentham's Panopticon.

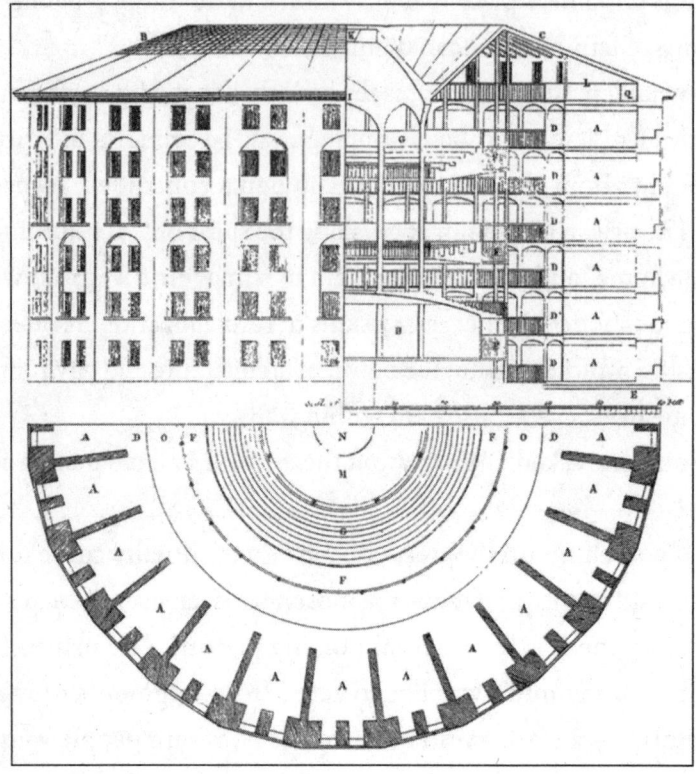

More than just a building, the Panopticon conceived by the English social reformer Jeremy Bentham had faith in the idea that architecture itself could be a tool for moral reform. In 1791, he introduced his design: a prison layout that was circular, with cells arranged in a ring around a central guard tower. Bentham's design was deceptively simple yet psychologically sophisticated. Every cell faced inward, toward the watchtower at the center, yet the guard tower was shrouded, its occupants hidden from view. This meant that while guards could observe the prisoners, the prisoners could never see their watchers. Each incarcerated person would be left to wonder if they were being watched at any given moment, creating a state of perpetual surveillance—or rather, the impression and anxiety of it.

Bentham's goal was not to fortify walls or limit movement purely for security, but to instill a constant self-awareness in the prisoners, an unrelenting consciousness that someone could be observing them at any time. It was a psychological model of control made possible through the visual sight lines of the architectural building itself. He believed that this ever-present watchfulness would prompt inmates to internalize authority, guiding them toward self-regulation and ultimately reform. In Bentham's mind, notably, this structure also demanded something from the theoretical warden. The structure would expose the warden's actions and make him or her accountable to those under watch. In practice the latter has proven to be a faulty assumption, but this shared responsibility is in fact what prevented the empowered classes from accepting the Panopticon into prisons and workplaces sooner.

Though Bentham's original plans were not fully realized on a large scale during his life, the idea resonated with prison designers for centuries. By the nineteenth century, this model of watchfulness became synonymous with prison architecture and reform. Oslo's original Central Prison, built in a circular panoptic shape and where Høidal had originally learned his trade, is just one of many institutions like it—utilizing a spatial "technology" proposed by a single person's theory.

I'd first read about the Panopticon in Michel Foucault's seminal 1975 book *Discipline and Punish: The Birth of the Prison*. Foucault saw the Panopticon as a metaphor for power, extending Bentham's architectural principle into a broader critique of modern society that he calls Biopower. Not merely meant to enforce order, these spaces, in Foucault's reading, were designed to normalize authoritarian behavior, instill discipline, and enforce conformity.

Foucault's Panopticon signals a shift in the nature of power: from sovereign power, which was exercised publicly and violently (e.g., executions and torture), to disciplinary power, which is invisible, continuous, and ingrained in everyday life. The brilliance here lies in its subtlety. It turns the observed into the observers—not of their own overseer but of each other through an internalized self-discipline. People become "docile bodies," molded to fit the expectations of the institutions that govern them.

Foucault's theory is one of how architectures shape our behavior without our self-awareness. It is an argument that if we are looking for how power operates in a society, we should look at the buildings themselves to see the invisible systems of power operating in very visible, material ways. All around us and at all times.

This, I realized, is why even though I had not spent much time visiting prisons in my life, it was a powerful testing ground for how my work had interacted with even the most subterranean elements of existence. In this way, the prison—even if we never have the misfortune to be committed to one—shapes each of our lives and the life of the societies we are citizens in.

The Panopticon was in its time celebrated as a revolutionary step toward prison reformation. But by the twentieth century, the Panopticon came to symbolize something far darker: the capacity of surveillance to strip people of autonomy, identity, and dignity.

As prisons became more widespread, they embodied increasingly punitive methods of control. In Nazi Germany, Albert Speer, Hitler's chief architect, was responsible for concentration camps like Mauthausen, strategically placed near quarries to extract prisoner labor for monumental Nazi building projects. Elsewhere in occupied Poland, camps such as Auschwitz-Birkenau, Treblinka, and Belzec served as both labor camps and death factories. As Viktor Frankl described, these were made up of "long stretches of several rows of barbed wire fences; watch towers; search lights; and long columns of ragged human figures, grey in the greyness of dawn, trekking along the straight desolate roads, to what destination we did not know." These sites were not merely places of imprisonment but of unimaginable brutality—where starvation, torture, and mass murder were carried out with chilling efficiency. Worse still, they became laboratories for experiments testing the limits of human endurance and the capacity for pain, reducing prisoners to subjects under constant observation and control.

Viktor Frankl, a trained psychotherapist, recounts his own experience surviving the conditions of Auschwitz in his seminal classic *Man's Search for Meaning.* He described the prison conditions as so totalizing that "If the man in the concentration camp did not struggle against this in a last effort to save his self-respect, he lost the feeling of being an individual, a being with a mind, with inner freedom and personal value. He thought of himself then as only a part of an enormous mass of people; his existence descended to the level of animal life."

Or put more bluntly to me, as one resident recalled, "If you treat us like animals, we will act like animals."

The architecture of such facilities mirrored the psychological devastation they inflicted. Constant observation robbed individuals of privacy and eroded any sense of self. The Panopticon's premise—that relentless surveillance could reform behavior—was exposed as profoundly flawed. Instead of fostering rehabilitation, these environments bred isolation and paranoia. Those within were separated from their very humanity. Observation might compel compliance, but it was also stultifying.

In Norway, this new wave of prison reformers was asking a set of bold questions, with Halden at its center.

While observation remained a necessary element, light-filled spaces, communal areas, and access to education and meaningful work were woven into the architecture to create a sense of normalcy for the imprisoned. Opponents argued this approach was unnecessary or took more attention than absolutely required, but Halden's architects and reformers believed (and showed through evidence) that by nurturing human dignity, they could reduce recidivism and create safer societies. The theory goes that careful work inside the prison will pay itself forward to the outside world.

———

Halden's sense of renewal went through and through, right down to its bones (architecture) and DNA (staff).

Every guard, we were told, was trained for this kind of prison. Only after a period to establish a new culture within Halden would former guards of other facilities be brought in and asked to adapt. It was not just that redesigning the space was necessary to focus on the individual's dignity and capability as a human, but it was also a way to adjust the culture of the guards and the correctional officers.

One specific strategy was to focus on the guard-to-resident ratio. In Bentham's Panopticon drawing from 1790, prisoners were kept in individual cells encircling a guard tower. There were twenty-four rooms per floor and six floors. However, since the floors were all open to the singular guard tower, the singular guard was the all-seeing authoritarian eye. Because of this, I would label this a 1/144 ratio, or one guard to 144 subjects.

Later prison designs took this method and evolved it. The Pennsylvania system, based on Quaker ideals of a reform through silence, reflection, and repentance, aimed to rehabilitate through a form of silent retreat or solitary confinement. John Haviland designed the Eastern State Penitentiary in the early nineteenth century as a spoke-and-wheel layout with a central guard station (similar to the Panopticon), but in place of a circular perimeter were seven rectangular housing blocks made from long hallways (double-loaded) with cells on either side. Each prisoner had his own exercise yard outside, with high walls so they could not communicate with other prisoners. And each cell had one single glass window in the ceiling. The "eye of God" skylight suggested to the prisoners that God was the one surveilling their every movement.

This design, while also keeping prisoners isolated, had the supposed benefit of reducing staffing, sometimes having as few as one guard per block of thirty-eight rooms. A 1/38 ratio. But without a doubt, the lower the ratio the better the outcome.

Seduced by the "efficiency," this layout influenced prison design around America and the world, many adopting a method of prioritized solitary confinement. However, over time, the psychological toll of solitary confinement on the whole became clear as prisoners subjected to it exhibited severe mental health issues, including depression, anxiety, and hallucinations. The intended reformist impacts of rehabilitation through penitence were overshadowed by the toll of social deprivation.

A shift was made to another American innovation in prison design, the Auburn system, which shifted the total isolation of the Pennsylvania system to allow for communal collective work and labor from the prisoners. The Auburn model—designed for Auburn Correctional Facility in New York state—took mass warehousing to a new level. Instead of each room getting its own window to the outside, the Auburn model packed a four-story tower of cells inside a large shell structure. The collective space was meant to be used for working together, but strict silence was enforced. This required more guards while prisoners were working together and more observation, but fewer when locked in their cells. And it influenced major prisons in the US—like Alcatraz (now a museum) and San Quentin, which is still using the Auburn-style prison today.

The guard-to-prisoner ratio of the Auburn model was high, however, because it forced more of the prison population to be locked away at a given time. Today the San Quentin prison employs this model to have up to as many as two hundred inmates watched over by a single correctional officer.

But in Halden, the ratio was extremely low, 1/10. Each block was ten rooms. Two staff members would observe from a control booth on the floor that could see into two units at once and was a visible and transparent (shatterproof) room that looked like a welcome desk. When Høidal took us to visit, the residents sat with us and cooked us a meal with the utensils, knives, and cooking implements they'd all been granted access to use. They each had generous access to light, with big picture windows onto the yard. Not exactly the eye of God, or the Auburn rooms, which had no windows at all, just a view of the open world beyond their four walls. It was clear that the smaller the ratio, the better the outcomes.

———

As I absorbed the experience of Halden, I thought about this base structure of cells, celled architecture (be it the prison cell, the hospital room, or the municipal housing block), and all the ways in which this model can atomize us into identical units, without difference, without character or identity, and without say. The cell is a way to imagine we all need and can be sustained by the same thing. It's an approach that dehumanizes us into an imaginary average without voice or identity.

Even within this sameness of the institution, subjectivity experiences differ. Protective and forced isolation are methods well documented and abused in American prisons, where some are forced to live in solitary confinement for years, without recourse. Vast evidence shows how destructive isolation can be to the mind through withering, radical desocialization. Nevertheless, Halden still has isolation units to address safety concerns inside.

"So what happens when violence occurs in the prison?"

This was a topic that had not been volunteered during the review of Halden. The genuinely encouraging discussions of reform and liberation had been a powerful introduction, but now one member of our group was determined to poke holes in all we'd seen. Høidal was not surprised by the query, as if it's the first question he gets in every discussion. He remained confident in his replies. "For those who cannot live with others, we have a specialized unit. There are also isolation cells, but these are available for prisoners to opt into voluntarily—a kind of silent retreat."

The murmur arose around the room at the term *silent retreat*. In the US it is called the Shoe, and it is anything but voluntary. "Most residents will eventually work outside the prison walls," Høidal explained, "and all will be reintegrated. The average sentence is about eight months. Even with a life sentence, the maximum here is twenty-one years."

Smirks swept through the room. Twenty-one years? In the United States, twenty-one years is often a standard sentence for serious offenses like manslaughter or assault. Life without parole is common, and the death penalty remains an unspoken reality for others.

I wondered about Anders Breivik, a Norwegian far-right extremist who at the time of our visit had very recently murdered seventy-seven people—most of them teenagers—during the 2011 Utøya Island massacre, one of the deadliest lone-wolf attacks in modern history.

I opened my mouth and raised the matter and the room stilled. Høidal's deputy, Jan Strømnes, a tall and measured counterbalance to Høidal's buoyant charisma, paused before responding. His face tightened. Tears welled in his eyes as he considered his response.

Clearly, this was not the first time he'd faced this challenge to the task all the prison's workers had taken on. To be honest, my question had been more provocative than insightful, knowing that Breivik's name loomed over everything regarding the nation's prison system that we had been exploring that day. And yet Strømnes responded with grace.

Life behind bars is possible in Norway, he shared, with consecutive life sentences, but it required a thorough review process after each twenty-one-year sentence. There was a presumption of reform, not a presumption of perpetual danger.

His voice softened and he said, "And unlike the United States, we do not have the death penalty."

Norway abolished the death penalty in the 1970s, joining a broader European trend. West Germany, for instance, outlawed capital punishment in 1949 with the adoption of the Basic Law, which enshrines the right to human dignity—a principle born out of the horrors of World War II.

When Bryan Stevenson spoke about the death penalty, he often described a conversation he had with a German scholar. The scholar told him, "There's no way, with our history, we could ever engage in the systematic killing of human beings. It would be unconscionable for us to, in an intentional and deliberate way, set about executing people."

In Stevenson's framing, the scholar had been correct. "What would it feel like to live in a world where the nation-state of Germany was executing people, especially if they were disproportionately Jewish?" Stevenson asked. "I couldn't bear it . . . And yet, in this country, in the states of the Old South, we execute people . . . in the very states where there are buried in the ground the bodies of people who were lynched."

In the 1970s, these two cultures, Germany and the United States, went through a wrenching period of confrontation and self-assessment, watching the results trickle down into their systems of criminal justice. Germany took up reform, and while reformers and activists attempted new systemic experiments in the 1970s, the United States—for reasons both too obvious and others all too complex for me to attempt to summarize in short form here—took the opposite route. As of 1970, the US population of imprisoned people was around 200,000. Today, it exceeds 1.8 million.

As Stevenson reminded us in his 2012 speech, these statistics came with a shocking racial disparity, where "one in three Black men between the ages of eighteen and thirty is in jail, in prison, on probation, or parole." This thirst for mass incarceration fueled an explosion in prison construction, reshaping not only American landscapes but its cultural ethos.

For so long, I had taken the brutal realities of American prisons as immutable: The architecture of despair that made up these structures of imprisonment, the hopelessness and lack of care I'd been inundated with and made to believe as a citizen here were inevitable, even appropriate. And then the utter privilege to see this alternative model, this hopeful revolution in reform through architecture. It was like a lighthouse leading us out of the fog of the impossible, toward full system reformation.

I felt easily that no architecture had been so transformative to me. Its vision was the built manifestation of a belief in outcomes that were *hoped for*, instead of predetermined. The others on the trip were changed as well. A state senator from South Carolina, Gerald Malloy, returned determined to introduce legislation inspired by Halden's principles. A warden from Massachusetts and another from Connecticut left with plans to pilot new programs in their facilities. Leann Bertsch, then North Dakota's director of corrections and rehabilitation, came back with a mission to "implement our humanity" in her state's prisons, pushing for autonomy and dignity to become central tenets. Kevin Kempf, then Idaho's corrections director, was equally struck. "We came back totally converted," he said.

One of the most compelling transformations, however, was that of Scott Semple, Connecticut's Department of Correction commissioner at the time. Inspired by both Halden's and Germany's systemic changes, Scott returned and established the TRUE Unit (Truthfulness, Respectfulness, Understanding, and Elevating) at Cheshire Correctional Institution.

Scott invited me and my colleague Jeffrey Mansfield to visit his TRUE Unit, contained within the fortresslike prison that allowed its arrival as a testing ground inside, a maze of byzantine hallways opened into the unit, a triangular dormitory originally built decades ago and now transformed to house fifty individual rooms spread over two levels, all centered on a shared common space.

Modest but private, each room opened into this shared area now stocked with functional yet sparse furniture and a library filled with books. There was a small computer lab for video calls, a barbershop took over one of the cells, and even a laundry room inserted—simple amenities that were revolutionary adaptations in this setting.

One resident told me he hadn't done his own laundry in twenty years before moving to this unit. Others shared that they hadn't prepared a meal or had meaningful control over their environment in decades. This dorm was experimenting with autonomy and normalcy, allowing residents to paint their rooms, tend a shared garden, and engage in activities that restored a sense of agency. It wasn't perfect—outside, the yard was little more than dirt and grass with a basketball court—but even the small changes felt monumental in their impact.

My eyes passed over the environment and took notice of the furniture, still mostly designed specifically for prisons, and its institutional coldness stood out even more now. Known as "behavioral health furniture," it was anti-ligature to prevent suicide, weighted to avoid being used as a weapon, and indestructible. And in the renovated space, next to the cold metal bookshelves, one of the principles of the designers' approach to Halden was differentiating between "soft" and "hard" spaces and materials. Domestic spaces were soft, while intake spaces were hard. In the American prison, all spaces and furniture were hard and looked institutional and inhospitable.

"Could we use even softer materials on the furniture?" I asked Scott, recalling Halden's comfortable couches and Danish chairs.

"The code doesn't allow it, but we could look into it in the TRUE unit," Scott said.

TRUE's work went far beyond furniture, as important as it was. Mentorship programs paired older residents serving life sentences with younger, more disruptive individuals to mediate conflict and foster accountability. Guards and residents alike were encouraged to engage with dignity and mutual respect.

Our conversation meandered into the notion that some of the biggest allies for this reform were the guards themselves. These spaces were so oppressive that correctional officers had high rates of turnover, alcoholism, and mental health needs. If an emphasis was put on the idea that prisons are workplaces, too, and that COs and residents all deserve better, that care would translate to the kind of support COs are able to provide to the residents. One former guard, we learned, had asked residents for a second chance to see him differently, promising to change his behavior just as the prison as a whole was promising to rethink its presentation of living space to its inhabitants. This act of vulnerability was being made possible only now, within a culture that invited mutual respect.

While in the unit, I helped conduct a drawing exercise, though I soon learned that architectural plans like those I solicited were considered contraband in prisons—a relic of paranoia that imagined any knowledge of the building's layout as a potential escape tool. Still, the residents' sketches showed a real demand for the addition of humane design, elements like gardens, outdoor spaces, and even sanctuaries for retreat and reflection. Their visions called for autonomy and access to normal life, rejecting the stark, defensive aesthetics of their surroundings. These prisoners had not seen what I had at Halden, but their imaginations aligned clearly with what had been made a reality an ocean away.

What was more pronounced than at Halden, however, was a consistent request for safety. In the US, prisoners had been subjected to frequent acts of violence, whether inflicted upon themselves or conducted in the spaces they were asked to live in afterward. They asked for more security and more correctional officers (a higher ratio) to make their daily lives safer and allow the residents to work toward a more humane, integrated culture of responsibility and accountability.

A little bit more trust could make all the difference. And from my experience as a designer, I knew that by activating our senses, these spaces could be transformed to calm and protect those living within them. The lessons from deinstitutionalization hospitals could be applied here, too. If simple views of nature and calm, comfortable settings could force patients to feel less stress, ask for less upon mediation, and be released much sooner—why wouldn't these same lessons work in the prison?

How could anyone expect human beings to improve and rehabilitate themselves in an environment that presented no hope and said, without word but with design, that the people here had no value or positive potential?

———

In every unique discipline there are system thinkers that break through the ordinary and blaze their own pathway. Farmer and Stevenson were certainly those figures, and while there are many in the prison reform movement, one of the brightest lights is Reginald Dwayne Betts. Betts is an activist, author, and lawyer who had been doing his own work on prison reform, and when he started to reach out about putting into action his ideas and realized he needed designers, my name and the work of my team came up.

Dwayne reached out with his big idea of how to plant hope— freedom—inside every prison in America. He wanted to put a thousand libraries across the country in prisons in every state, all part of an initiative he called Freedom Reads.

———

Dwayne was formerly incarcerated himself and had been transformed by books and reading he had been able to do during his time in prison. It inspired him to get his undergraduate, master's, and law degrees, while becoming a published poet, author, playwright, podcaster, and MacArthur Award–winning visionary. He has extracted such power from the written word and knows that by making books accessible to all prisoners, he would surely see more successes similar to his own. But Betts wanted the books to be held on a shelf that could be more crafted than metal brackets that prisons specify. Freedom Reads needed to feel special and to attract the attention of those in prison he was able to connect with, so he reached out to me and my team for design assistance.

The project of designing a bookshelf at first blush might not "feel" transformative, but Dwayne saw a well-crafted and -designed shelf as a seed of beauty planted in the field so often devoid of life. He saw it as a Trojan horse that would change perception, change policy, and lift hope, much like the books it held were designed to display.

My colleagues Regina Yang and John Mayer jumped into this work feetfirst. We designed bookshelves in the shape of a simple

S-curve—an arc—so that they could be accessed on either side and wheeled into different locations within any space, creating different zones. Multiple shelves could be assembled to delineate a circular reading room or a curvilinear room divider. The shelves would be made from solid wood like maple, walnut, cherry, or oak, handcrafted with handmade joints, and finished in a reflective varnish. The arc shape contrasts the straight lines of the prison and reminded Dwayne of a Martin Luther King Jr. quote, "The arc of the moral universe is long but it bends towards justice." These were bent bookshelves.

———

We knew the bookshelves would be a key to unlocking a different story in the prison space. They would be an example of careful, human-forward design and would employ more soft and natural materials that could be used in other places as well. It was an attempt to disrupt by systems hacking—a design intervention that would make us see all the designs around us in a new light by raising a simple question, "If we can have *this*, then why should we settle for *that*?" Dwayne went about finding prisons to put them in, and by August 2025 he'd completed five hundred Freedom Reads libraries around the country—a simple but radical start to a revolution through reading.

———

Redesigning anything in prisons is fraught with complexity. It requires navigation of a minefield of ethical debates, reputational risks, and systemic constraints. Conversations get mired in virtue signaling and skepticism from potential partners. And the hesitation is understandable: The United States has a scale of incarceration the system was never designed to handle. To return to a more humane and comparable level, we'd need to claw back to the incarceration rates before the 1970s boom. Nevertheless, many want prison abolished completely and posit that against this backdrop, any attempt to tinker within the system can feel complicit in perpetuating a racist, dehumanizing, and often murderous structure.

Because of this, many architects refuse outright to work on prison-related projects. A broader cultural movement within architecture called out firms involved in the "justice industry," with public shaming campaigns targeting designers who contributed to prisons, particularly those creating execution chambers or solitary confinement cells. But *any* work on prisons placed those involved at risk of being denounced by vocal reformers. Activists successfully pressured the American Institute of Architects (AIA) to adopt a policy against designing in these facilities. For some, any engagement short of full abolition was a betrayal.

The abolitionist perspective draws heavily on thinkers like Angela Davis, whose seminal work "Are Prisons Obsolete?" positions incarceration as an extension of slavery. For abolitionists, the very concept of prison is irredeemable—a structure inherently tied to systemic oppression. This absolutism has fueled vibrant activism but also created deep divides. The debate isn't just philosophical; it often pits abolitionists against reformers in zero-sum terms: Is there still value in improving conditions within a system many see fit only for destruction?

These tensions came to a head during the No New Jails protests against New York City's plan to close Rikers Island. The proposed shift to smaller, borough-based jails aimed to improve conditions and bring incarcerated individuals closer to their families, but activists denounced the plan as reformist betrayal. Years of work to close Rikers—a notorious hub of abuse—were threatened by commitment to a perfect end. For families with loved ones still inside the system, the debates were of little use.

I found myself wrestling with these questions personally. Was I complicit in a broken system by engaging with its redesign? Or could meaningful change within the system alleviate suffering for millions? My experiences in Norway, where I saw a prison built on principles of dignity and rehabilitation, had shown me what was possible. I couldn't unsee it. I wrestled with this sense of absolutism around the topic—could we really let people languish in dehumanizing conditions while waiting for a utopian future of abolition?

This controversy came to a head during a panel discussion in Washington, DC, where I shared the stage with Dwayne Betts and Scott Semple as we prepared to announce the installation of a Freedom Reads library at the National Building Museum. Toward the end of the talk, an audience member stood to ask Dwayne, "Do you consider yourself to be a prison abolitionist or a prison reconstructionist?"

Dwayne tried to punt the question to me, but I demurred, feeling unequipped and at risk of the trap of the question, and then Betts picked it up, with a deep breath, acknowledging that he gets this question at nearly every lecture. He hesitated and then answered with the authority of someone who had lived through the system and had developed a nuanced understanding of suffering and hope. His voice carried the weight of personal experience.

"I [do not] resent your question . . . but I resent the foundation of that question, because the foundation of that question asks me to display how I [care] about something that I have committed my life to, when I wake up every day in a country . . . with peers, with colleagues, with neighbors who would deny me employment, housing, an education, because I robbed somebody." He paused, scanning the room. "When I go to Angola prison, nobody asks me if I'm an abolitionist. They ask me, 'Do you believe I should be free—despite the fact that I killed somebody?' Some of the questions we ask of me, of anybody who has been incarcerated, we should be asking of ourselves."

The moral courage, Dwayne seemed to say, was not to

acknowledge and signal that you know about the system, but to work toward any change with the tools at your disposal. Architecture was my tool, and I could foresee no more urgent architecture to reimagine than the prison. Dwayne's words gave me renewed confidence in the possibility of my work bringing positive change to a very broken element of our society, but the experience did force me to wonder, with my work, whether the narrative story between liberation and sublimation was being weaponized too easily within the same community, pushing allies to the fringes and scaring potential advocates from engaging in the difficult moral questions it demands of us.

At the core of the inquiry is possibly asking the right question. It may not be: How to design a better prison? But rather: What ways do the authoritarian principles (made so evident in the architecture of prisons) find their way into our everyday spaces of living, learning, and working, and whether it is ever achievable.

The architect Giancarlo De Carlo mused about these very aspirations, writing in 1969 about how institutions—like the prison—reproduce themselves to preserve class and social hierarchy. To deinstitutionalize begins not with a different design, but with changing the design process itself to be more collective and democratic—to seek voice and participation in the constituents it serves. He notes, "It should be assumed as an ultimate goal which could become real, that in the future the process of planning the physical environment can be entirely governed by the collectivity [. . .] At that point the ambiguous and insidious function of the specialists (of the architect) will be deprived of all authority. But that point is a long way off and how long it will take to reach it depends [. . .] on how quickly the exercise of freedom will be able to destroy the barriers of alienation which the exercise of power has erected."

Design might be my tool, but some problems are too vast and indecipherable and enormous to be completed. In those cases they become walls to chip away at or relay races to jump into. The prison is such a system, where each era of reform is both idealist and complicit. Both humane and inhumane. But at the core is a truth that I learned from my work with both Dr. Paul and Mr. Stevenson, that what happens inside prisons is not isolated from the conditions in which we live—comfortably in our homes and communities. We may believe we are free, but the reality is that our lives are bound to the conditions of confinement endured by others. The prison may be hidden, but it is tethered to us. It functions as a mirror, reflecting back on the structures, values, and inequities we collectively uphold. "The true measure of our character," Bryan Stevenson has reminded us, "is how we treat the poor, the disfavored, the accused, the incarcerated, and the condemned."

At Halden, the redesign was possible because the government approached the project not from a building standpoint but from a system redesign position. Halden is just the physical manifestation of that white paper, that aspirational reimagined system.

In the US, where punitive systems sit next to rehabilitative ones, an overarching redesign remains far from our grasp, despite the efforts of many great advocates for many years. And yet, the correctional officers, themselves seeing the difference between a dangerous workplace they must defensively enter and the condition of confinement where residents and staff work collaboratively toward reintegration, have begun to make profound headway into changing the carceral state. A different breed of organizer—built from labor unions fighting to improve the working conditions for correctional officers, have organized walk-offs and wholesale stop-work orders. These officers have pushed for safe and humane working conditions for those inside the system. It continues to be one of many examples where spaces of labor, powered by collective organizations, changed workplaces—usually the factories and the offices, but now the prisons—and turned them into spaces where social movements and social change became possible.

Chapter 8

THE WORKPLACE

Boston, Massachusetts

For all of us, 2020 was a monumental year. The COVID pandemic had started to ripple across the world in late January, just as my wife and I welcomed our first child, and right before my fortieth birthday. We retreated to my in-laws' home in Maine to soak in those precious moments, but also to shelter from the sickness everyone was showing up to work with, a virulence we were only starting to understand.

At that time, our office was a typical layout of the age—an open plan. The office had by that time grown and moved into an old brick building on Boylston Street in Boston, spanning three interconnected structures with mismatched floor levels; we shared the space with a few other like-minded organizations. Rows of desks filled the central bay, with conference rooms ringing the perimeter. Natural light filtered in through old, drafty windows—two on either side of the space—which were often left open for ventilation without much thought to what that actually meant.

The open layout, while it did encourage interaction, also amplified distractions. Noise traveled unimpeded, whether it was a colleague fielding a client call or the booming sound of cars outside. For an entire summer, there was even a guy standing on our corner dressed in a tricorn hat and Revolutionary War uniform playing a piccolo, working for change. Boston is a city of piercing nostalgia.

Employees donned noise-canceling headphones as armor against the cacophony, a visual symbol of the delicate balance between connection and focus. It was far from a perfect situation.

This "open plan" had been a point of tension in ours and other workplaces. While it allowed for spontaneous collaboration—ideas sparked in passing conversations or impromptu desk-side meetings—it also made deep, focused work difficult. Between the bright screens, Slack dings, Facebook likes, and constant stream of email, the creative mind space we needed to carve out in order to produce quality work was under increasing attack from the physical space of the office. Distraction-free enclosures and focus space were essential for the creative economy emerging out of the Great Recession. However, that same economy was also reshaping labor itself, making work bleed into any and all spaces real and digital, and at all times. The culture of working changed, too, where workplaces became cultures in themselves, enclosed ecosystems of habits, team dynamics, and shared belief systems, increasingly untethered from the spaces that had been designed to produce them. The architecture could not keep up with these evolutionary shifts and specific labor needs in these distracting times. When COVID struck, the cracks in the dam holding this fragile ecology together seemed to finally break.

———

The pandemic brought a great deal of truth to the axiom "the only power against capital is labor power." That without it, or even with it, capital will find a way. And that even while capital can incentivize, it by nature will also alienate (as Marx would write) and treat workers as the masses: nameless automatons, separated from their agency, in the service of capital power. Units of commerce to be protected or sacrificed when it came down to it.

COVID made clear that the modern labor floor, like the factory floor past, was both alienating and empowering. Workers mobilized through the factory, not in spite of it, and contemporary work floor plans had a way of quieting down any calls for collective action.

Unions, to be fair, operated upon this same pressure system as well. The 51 percent rule, whereby a 51 percent vote of the workforce can form a union that then negotiates for all workers, at once empowered the workforce while also compelling them to pay dues for a membership they did not personally desire. But when the company was an invulnerable king, right-to-work laws had already tried to detangle this financial vehicle and power leverage by turning workers against one another and claiming some were more equal than others. So what then of the new era of disaggregated work and asynchronous labor? I wondered, how does the space of the factory, the space of the workplace, activate or alienate, empower or extract?

De Carlo, the theorist-cum-architect I mentioned earlier, had considered this tension, too. He had argued we needed to change the design process and work *with* labor to design their own houses. His Urbino Project in Italy was a case study of participatory engaged design where the architect was not giving a design but designing hand in hand with the laborers' needs and aspirations top of mind. He was mostly successful, changing the timbre of relationships between the city, its capital class, its inhabitants, and the government. But in the United States we still had much to learn.

This was part of the reason why I had set up our firm as a nonprofit organization and called it a collective. I thought the configuration was such that through distributed leadership, empowered voices, and encouraging collaborative work experiences, we could shift the role of the architect to be allied partner, not speaker. To some degree this worked, for a while.

The superpower, I would say, of the nonprofit configuration is that it was not "owned" by anyone. I did not own it, and the board of directors were mere stewards of it. This configuration, I thought, was a check and balance against the tyranny of design leadership and could encourage a sense of worker buy-in, that we were in it together. But ownership can be a potent tool as well in community work. True ownership creates shared accountability and skin in the game. And without equity in the business, Jo Freeman tells us in her famous 1971 essay, "The Tyranny of Structurelessness," power centers emerge regardless of intent through other forms of authoritarian hierarchy, be it status, credit, or identity, instead of shares and percentages.

The nonprofit center is a powerful model and can introduce important questions at the core of work and partnership. But no model can truly resist authoritarian power, Freeman tells us. It is not something that dissipates with a structure or idealism, it simply shifts in its form and character, and so any configuration needs careful tending and collective honest interrogation.

The nonprofit is at heart aspirational and optimistic, but there was always a worry that this distributed system might lead to a hesitation in design—a lack of voice. A sense that decisions were not *made* but *agreed upon by committee*. I wanted to believe that we could redesign our practice to correct for this concern as well. And now we were venturing into parts even more unknown.

———

My first flight back from paternity leave came early in the outbreak, in March 2020, when we were unaware of how dramatic it would be. It was a trip to Los Angeles for a lecture at USC's School of Architecture. Our bubble—the one protecting our newborn from any potential sickness—had become increasingly fragile, and the plane ride felt as reckless as it could be.

At LAX, the terminal was unlike those I had spent the last ten years living in. It was sparsely populated, with an eerie hush replacing the usual din of human activity that soundtracks an international airport. The flight I had taken was empty, and I stood out as one of the few wearing a protective mask—a precaution rooted in my history with airborne disease research. Information on what we were facing was still scarce, but my instincts and newborn were enough to self-protect, and sure enough as I landed news was breaking that there had been an outbreak traced back to that very terminal.

When I got there, the lecture hall at USC was nearly empty as well, and whether the poor turnout was my own lack of appeal as a lecturer or a growing anxiety around public gatherings seemed to matter little. It was tense in that room. As I began to speak and present stories of tuberculosis hospitals designed to mitigate disease and cities decimated by diseases like cholera, I paused from my prepared remarks with an "aha" moment. "Do you see the air now?" I gestured to the space around us, pointing to the air above us. "I see it now, pressing upon us, threatening me in a way I never noticed before." COVID had made that invisible spatial scourge visible. The air around us, and how we breathe, these very spaces we inhabited were now threats, and the very act of our breathing was tied to our ability to be protected within them. I flew home, and like the rest of the country (and world), my team and I shut down our office to move to remote and online work, part of the swell of the never-before-seen era of a fully remote workplace.

The Wainwright Building in Saint Louis, Missouri
Courtesy of Library of Congress

The modern office building is the apotheosis of Louis Sullivan's mantra, "form ever follows function." In designing the Wainwright Building in St. Louis (1891), Sullivan's goal was to create a space for a brewers' association, but his innovation would be what is known as the first skyscraper. It was tall and took up an entire city block and soared upward. But perhaps unexpectedly now, it was also a boxy, flat-roofed structure, with deep, open floor plates for desks. The design was not completely austere either. Sullivan covered the outside in hues of terra-cotta and sandstone. The building resembled a classical Greek column, which traditionally had three distinct sections. The ground floor (base) was for retail, the middle floors (the shaft) were similar in layout with open floor plans for offices, desks, and workers, and the top area (the capital) was a layer of ornamental terra-cotta frieze, would hide the mechanical systems of the elevator and water tanks for fire suppression.

Sullivan's project was heralded as its own innovation stylistically, but how it functions, its use—that of an office space made up of large floor plans of desks and offices—had as much to do with the industrial factories of the nineteenth century as it did with the evolving innovations of steel frame construction that allowed for taller and wider buildings. It was a new type of vertical factory leaping from its industrial origins.

The industrial factory worked much like a math equation. What is the largest number of people who can be squeezed onto a floor designed to produce products, at higher yields, in competitively faster times, and with the equipment necessary to produce them? In many conditions, ornament and aesthetics were applied; no structure is fully devoid of them, but the overall outcome is a form that is "functional," and its purpose is to produce, through volume and yield, more output. The resultant structures were raw, pure, simplified articulations of the needs that industries required and driven by the incentives of capital to maximize profit and reduce inefficiencies of labor.

Not surprisingly, these floor plans mediate some of the contrasting interests of industry and the capital that forms them. On the one hand, spaces were needed to support workers and their health, and on the other, the factory floor plan was an extractive engine for labor and products. The clearest example of how this system can be abusive or extractive was the Triangle Shirtwaist Factory disaster of 1911 in New York City. The factory was a tenant in the Asch Building, a neo-Renaissance-style structure similar to the Wainwright Building in its form and tripartite articulation. The owners, the "shirtwaist kings," Max Blanck and Isaac Harris, overcrowded the floors and locked their exit doors to deter breaks by their seamstresses. When a fire broke out, the largest labor disaster in American history ensued, killing 146 workers. The tragedy prompted local and national outcry and fueled local unions and labor organizers to demand improvements in policy around workers' rights, as well as architectural and spatial improvements in building safety measures and requirements for fire mitigation, appropriate exits, occupancy loads, and design. These changes affected not just factories and office spaces but all building types, and emboldened labor rights organizers to push for national improvements in working conditions, pay, and the amenities associated with workplaces and jobs. As in so many disasters, building codes and spatial changes followed crisis.

As an old professor of mine, Neil Brenner, once reinforced for me, capital has so much disproportionate power that only organized and collective labor can be powerful enough to influence changes. Samuel Gompers called it social insurance, and Thomas Donahue (former AFL-CIO president) said, "The only effective answer to organized greed is organized labor."

Like with the prison rights movement, it was the conditions—the space and architecture—of the factory floor itself where these battle lines were formed and power over rights and representation, safety and health for all buildings, and social change were made possible, as a response to the decrepit conditions workers withstood until they could withstand it no longer.

But unlike the prison, which is cellular in design and solitary to restrict individuals from society and social conditions, the factory—the first open plan space—is communal, collective, and a society of its own. It is a social body with social norms, and social power when organized and activated. So while the factory is a manifestation of industry and its potential for alienation and extraction, the factory floor and the open floor plan are also a stage for culture and collective agency. Hence, why labor unions became such a foundational nucleus of power for much of the nineteenth and twentieth centuries in factory spaces.

———

The classic mill was rarely built in existing cities; instead, cities formed around the mills. Industry, on bodies of limitless water-power, were the impetus to settle people, labor, then commerce and culture. My hometown of Poughkeepsie was founded this way, as were many manufacturing centers of the northeast United States. First the mill, then the mill town, then the city.

I learned to see these political and social changes in the building—to read the building differently—when asked to think through the restoration of a nineteenth-century factory in North Adams, Massachusetts, a site of a textile mill that was being reimagined for modern use.

I met a visionary entrepreneur named Ben Svenson, who sought to transform a derelict motel and the old textile mill into a hotel. At the core of his vision was taking people away from the blaring ca-cophony of the city and the digital world by giving people a way to reengage with the land and with real places by having real experiences again. He and his partners saw this ignored corner of this fringe town as filled with potential and conceived of a project called Tourists as the center of a hospitality enterprise that could highlight the beauty of real life and pull us back to it. With hindsight, it proved to be a prescient vision.

The mill building was unique for its time, primarily for its functional aesthetic with touches of brick detail that showed the care taken for how it would appear from the street. The building spanned a river, or rather a man-made spur of the adjacent Hoosic River, which flowed through large circular chutes beneath the building to generate hydroelectric power for the sewing machines.

The building itself was also a marvel. It claimed large windows to filter light deep into what architects call its floor plate, the grounds for workers. A nineteenth-century factory is, in a way, a study in technology, asking how far we can span and how large floor plates can be (or how many people can one hold) while still allowing light to hit desks and air to move through. These were designs optimized for worker productivity, observation, and volume, in factories designed for mechanization, or the human equivalent of it.

The mill also revealed changes in social and labor policy. Amid the generous light pouring in from the windows were two means of egress and fire stairs that signal the changes in building code mandated by laws enacted by the Massachusetts Factory Act and reforms after the Triangle Shirtwaist Fire tragedy, such as the NFPA life safety code of 1927 and the Fair Labor Standards Act of 1938.

Other environmental issues around pollution of the adjacent Hoosic River and its surroundings and capped superfund parking lot signaled ongoing pollution challenges that later fostered reforms like the 1970s Clean Water and Clean Air Acts, which created incentives and mandates for polluting industries to clean up their environmental messes.

Down the street—Massachusetts Avenue—was the hamlet of Blackinton, offering a prototypical "factory town" lined with churches, saloons, a library, the houses of workers, managers, and employees, and even a jail. With Union soldiers' uniforms on commission in the 1860s, the mill town became one of the wealthiest in the state and led to expansion, the spawning of more mills farther downriver, and the founding of the city of North Adams, a larger industrial urban center where the spurs of the river collide.

But economic shifts had been decimating since then, and North Adams had become one of the poorest parts of the region when Svenson took on the enormous task of linking the town's past with its hopefully more prosperous future. He and his colleagues purchased a number of houses in Blackinton village, and the mill, for pennies on the dollar.

This was all familiar to me coming from a mill town of my own. Poughkeepsie had its era of mill buildings (1800s–1870s) and its attempts at vertical development like in Chicago. What we'd experienced that didn't make it to North Adams was that mid-century boom when IBM came in.

Poughkeepsie had seen the new material innovations in steel and glass, as well as air-conditioning systems that allowed new mid-century factory floors to extend for huge areas without need for windows at every bay. It is no coincidence that America's cities rose at the same time technology untethered their buildings from these physical, historical limitations.

Designing the workplace shaped architectural styles as well. Unlike buildings like the aforementioned Wainwright, a new movement was dominated by minimalist de-ornamented buildings that revered and mimicked the aesthetics and materiality of factories, cars, steamships, and industry.

———

In the 1960s and 1970s, corporate empires reflecting this new phase grew. More people were needed; floors had to be made adaptable to allow for new employees and changing collaboration requirements instead of tables of sewing machines—white-collar workers needed phones and independent desks for sales calls. Robert Propst, an industrial designer with Herman Miller Furniture in Holland, Michigan, responded with an innovation that would revolutionize offices—the cubicle—which he called "the action office." His cubicle design was intended to create a more flexible, adaptable, and productive environment for office workers, and it soon became irresistible to those putting up office towers and laying office floors across the nation.

Propst was a self-proclaimed systems designer. And his action office was just that, a system that could adapt to any floor plan and any work team. The promise of the cubicle was its ambition to mediate an individual's world within the vastness (and banality) of the collective. The promise of this design, however, was predicated on the corporate entities' use of that tool, and instead, the cubicle became synonymous with the extraction of culture, as individuals were atomized into nameless desks in a labyrinth of automatons and endless punch card labor. Mike Judge's 1999 film *Office Space* satirized this feeling at the peak of the late-twentieth-century "dot-com era" economic boom, skewering corporate culture and office life with the depressing aesthetics of the office architecture at its center. Blaring fluorescent lights, dropped ceilings of pockmarked and stained mineral fiber, beige walls, gray carpets, endless cubicles, and soulless monotony.

"Not all organizations are intelligent and progressive," Propst said two years before he died in 2000. His concept had been transformed into "monolithic insanity." "Lots are run by crass people. They make little, bitty cubicles and stuff people in them. Barren, rathole places."

The office changed with the advent and spread of the laptop and "mobile" workspace. No longer did each worker require eighty square feet of space defined by Propst's cubicle. Now shared desks and undefined workstations were common, without expectations of storage or personal space. The open-plan layout, free of cubicles, emerges again and dominates office design in the 2010s. Communal spaces became en vogue, attempting to encourage teamwork and transparency. Creative zones and "the big table" with "hot desking" started showing up in coworking tech spaces. A totalizing ecosystem of amenities, wellness, and comfort zones, casual and comfortable "turn off" areas, stocked fridges, and candy dispensers became normal perks.

These designs attempted to re-create a totalizing ecosystem for their labor, curating a culture for the company in ways not unlike what had been the purpose of the company town model of the early to mid-1900s. When the cubicle was deconstructed into collaborative work "zones," the labor environment took on a shape identical to the large floor plates of endless work areas and easy corporate surveillance that typified those mill town factory sites. And so earphones and digital communications started to pull us further into the cellular isolation of the collective digital sphere—a workplace that had not been designed for a different conception of how social networks work.

These designs, from the factory to the office park, to the flexible office of the digital age, were dividing labor from management and enabling panoptic ambition, a sense of constant monitoring while at work and a new form of alienation within the digital sphere.

———

Cal Newport's *Digital Minimalism* recounts how email shifted the way we work and the bleeding of work outside the hours of nine to five. Email, or what he refers to as asynchronous communication, which does not require both parties to be present at the same time, evolved from manageable to accretive with the totalizing effect of digital culture. Newport highlights how this new technology led to interruptions, fragmented attention, and increased stress at the workplace, and especially in creative work.

Newport's book (released right before the pandemic) advocates for more intentional use of email, social media, and screens, encouraging people to reduce their use and be aware of how these tools were using us, rather than being used intelligently and productively. Newport writes of this "attention economy" (psychologist Herbert Simon coined the term, calling it "a wealth of information [that] creates a poverty of attention") and its distractions, but his references were more timeless. He pointed to Henry David Thoreau's *Walden; or Life in the Woods* as the playbook for how to recapture focus and moral attention in a culture of distraction—by going back to nature. Thoreau's distractions in the second industrial era of the 1850s mill town of Concord, Massachusetts, were status accumulation, class pressure, and the moral ambiguities of a nation cleaved over slavery and its own conception of freedom. Jenny Odell also found nature emboldening in her 2020 book *How to Do Nothing* and called for us to witness what we spend time on and choose to do things aimlessly without knowing the reason or outcome—to suspend time, we had to choose a different way of working and way of being.

The workplace as we knew it in 2019 was already failing to accommodate the need for real, creative, thought-provoking work rather than digital busywork. And the architectural response was to recalibrate what we need and discard what we don't.

Personally, I had worried about these dynamics even before the pandemic forced us into a wholesale review, but our new reality hastened the cultural change many were already feeling. It was no longer just about noise or focus, distraction and collaboration—all issues we were facing at the workplace. Now it was also about survival, and about our families and their health. The culture around us was shifting, and the workplace was unequipped to handle it. And so the workplace transformed again, almost overnight, from the open-plan collaborative collective to the new cellularity, the cubicle of the digital era—on Zoom.

My wife's parents were artists, self-proclaimed back-to-the-land hippies who in another era of recalibration in the 1970s bought a raw plot of land in Freeport, Maine, and over a period of forty years built a rambling, creative family compound. When my wife and I drove back to Maine with our baby boy, not even two months old, we were determined to keep her parents' bubble intact and protect us and them. We would also be walking a well-worn path of searching for clarifying signals in the noise. It would be almost two years before the office was open for business again in an entirely transformed world.

———

Suddenly, the design of our environments was no longer a backdrop to life—it was everything. And the whole world finally started to see the truth in this as the office space disappeared and emptied— inessential as remote work from home took root—and the culture of work changed overnight. But essential workers, health-care and prison workers, and some schoolteachers stayed on the front lines and needed help navigating a new, poisonous workplace. In the maelstrom, we began to hear from leaders needing advice on how to rethink their workplaces while they navigated this new normal.

———

In April 2020, I got a call from John Bucuvalas, vice chair and professor of pediatrics at Mount Sinai Hospital in New York. "I have no idea if this is going to be good or lead to other problems," John Bucuvalas, a researcher at Mount Sinai Hospital in New York City, said to me when he called. "The canary in the coal mine," as he put it, "is health-care workers getting sick." If the doctors, nurses, and staff fell ill, the entire system would collapse.

COVID was peaking in New York City, and Mount Sinai was in the crosshairs. "They are redesigning the spaces on the fly," John said, and he asked if we could assist alongside them, to make sure we were helping these changes with spatial awareness in mind.

The outbreak had taken over the hospital, and the hallways were filled with equipment and stuff, while doctors and staff donned masks and full-body suits of personal protective equipment. They took off the masks in the break room, but the illnesses got passed on to each other and the patients, and the fear was palpable.

Amie Shao, one of our principals, and I had been called upon to confirm how their redesigns could be improved. I knew we could not enter the building, so we suggested a quick study where we would strap GoPro cameras to the heads of staff and monitor the floors. Meanwhile, we could analyze the floor plates through quick video calls with staff. We asked them to color which areas of the floor were safe or dangerous and which they were unsure about, using quick printouts of the fire exit plans on the walls and crayons from kids' rooms to show discrepancies of where the doctors' perceptions of clear or contaminated spaces appeared to be.

This was instructive for a few reasons. The spatial awareness was shifting. Staff were walking through spaces in full protective gear, and others were removing masks in spaces they deemed safe. Janitorial staff were walking through all the spaces inconsistent with strict protocols. The hospital wanted to ensure consistency and health.

These hospitals have outbreak contingency plans, and Mount Sinai instituted theirs. But the most telling hack was that doctors, rightly so, placed COVID patients in the "old" bed tower, built before World War II, where the windows were still operable. The newer bed towers had windows that could not open. The same logic of the factory and the office tower prevailed in the hospital, too: before air-conditioning, spaces had to be thinner and have access to fresh air from the world outside. When operability was no longer essential because of complex interior air-handling systems, the windows became aesthetic items only, portals to a natural view.

In many ways, the hospital had been anticipating a crisis like this all along. Innovations like negative pressure rooms, where air is siphoned out, and surgical suites that operate with HEPA-filtered air were already essential to protecting patients. But everyday spaces like hallways and waiting areas, being sealed under the same rubric of danger, were not prepared for the challenges of COVID. And bedrooms without access to operability revealed a flaw in airflow design of complex institutions—an overlooked need for air mixing and air changes per hour. Data points like volume of air and air exchange rates are the key drivers for how safe you will be if someone is sick, and there was not yet any way to collect those for the prevailing mass of the hospital. We had encountered similar challenges in Rwanda during the fight with tuberculosis, but this time the battlefield was in our most populous city and in one of the most advanced medical research institutions in the world.

———

The outbreak had pierced this technological marvel's logic and its capability. Despite near-infinite resources and layers of oversight, it was no longer able to provide for the most basic needs of its workers: safety and protection.

———

The study at Mount Sinai only reinforced what I had learned years ago: that buildings hold a critical space in shaping our health, and that their role in mediating access to the *right* to health places architecture and design into some more essential space I could not ever have anticipated back when I was just a student figuring out where I wanted to set my academic sails.

The order of things had been all wrong. Time had distanced practitioners from the core, baseline functions of the field. It was not principally about making beautiful buildings, nor about the right to healthfulness for those who inhabited those buildings. No, that was far too complicated for what this all came down to. The right to *breathe*, an even higher order, had been the fundamental driver all along. All the spaces around us, from factories to schools to hospitals to nursing homes to prisons, all of them workplaces, too, filled with essential workers, were hurting the people inside of them. And revealing where our built environment was fragile, incomplete, and designed without our right to breathe as the true priority.

———

By June, the world was completely different. The trauma and loss experienced came with a growing realization that we needed collective reckoning with the spaces around us. A great spatial awakening that all eight billion of us on this planet had been thrust into—seeing and feeling the buildings and spaces around us like never before, and asking questions about accessibility that had gone unexamined prior to this time. Had the spaces we inhabit and rely on really been created to care for and support the humans they contained? Was there a thoughtfulness about comfort and safety? And the general answer to those queries was: "We are not sure."

Like the changes the factory tragedies forced a century ago, I hoped new policies and new guidelines that were emerging would transform building standards to be more breathable and more flexible.

Michael P. Murphy Sr. repainting trim at the family home in Poughkeepsie, New York.
MICHAEL P. MURPHY JR.

Michael Murphy stands outside of his family home in Poughkeepsie, New York.
MICHAEL P. MURPHY JR.

Michael P. Murphy Sr. stands in a half-completed renovation project.
MICHAEL P. MURPHY JR.

Michael Murphy drawing the Butaro Hospital while a student at Harvard's Graduate School of Design.
MICHAEL P. MURPHY JR.

Locally–sourced volcanic rock used across the Butaro District Hospital campus in Rwanda.
IWAN BAAN

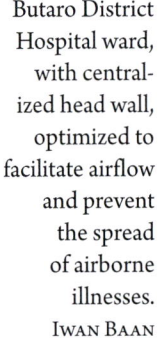

Butaro District Hospital ward, with central-ized head wall, optimized to facilitate airflow and prevent the spread of airborne illnesses.
IWAN BAAN

Butaro District Hospital, Rwanda (2011).
Iwan Baan

Butaro District Hospital's central courtyard, Rwanda.
IWAN BAAN

Michael Murphy, Bruce Nizeye, and Dr. Paul Farmer.
MICHAEL P. MURPHY JR.

Locally-sourced rock used across the Butaro District Hospital campus.
MICHAEL P. MURPHY JR.

The foundations of the Butaro District Hospital being excavated (2009).
MICHAEL P. MURPHY JR.

Michael Murphy presents early designs of the Butaro District Hospital to Rwanda (2008). Michael P. Murphy Jr.

Butaro District Hospital under construction. Michael P. Murphy Jr.

Hundreds of locals line up to begin working at the hospital. Michael P. Murphy Jr.

Interior waiting areas at GHESKIO Cholera Treatment Center, Port-au-Prince, Haiti (2015).
Iwan Baan

GHESKIO Cholera Treatment Center, Port-au-Prince, Haiti (2015).
Iwan Baan

GHESKIO Tuberculosis Hospital, Port-au-Prince, Haiti (2015).
Iwan Baan

Walkway Over the Hudson, Poughkeepsie, New York.
IWAN BAAN

Downtown Poughkeepsie, New York, overtaken by surface parking lots.
IWAN BAAN

The National Memorial for Peace and Justice, Montgomery, Alabama (2018).
Iwan Baan

The National Memorial for Peace and Justice, Montgomery, Alabama (2018).
Iwan Baan

The National Memorial for Peace and Justice, Montgomery, Alabama (2018).
Iwan Baan

Michael Murphy and Bryan Stevenson, executive director of Equal Justice Initiative, stand in front of the Soil Collection Community Remembrance Project.
MICHAEL P. MURPHY JR.

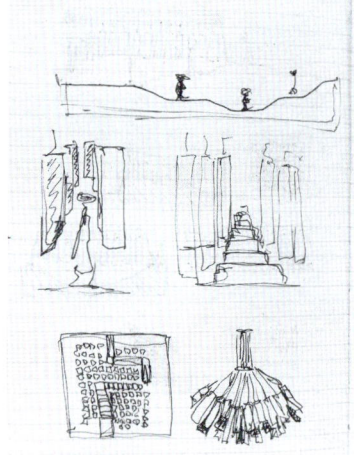

Early sketches for the National Memorial for Peace and Justice.
MICHAEL P. MURPHY JR.

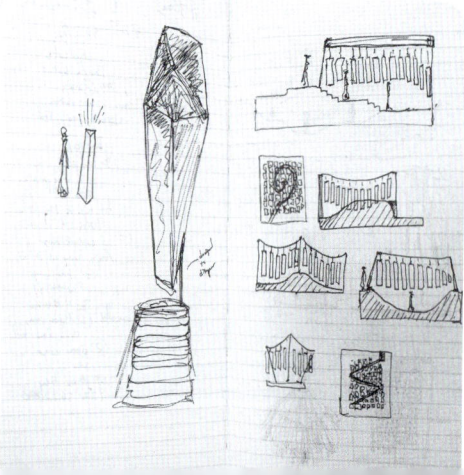

Michael Murphy and Dr. Paul Farmer at the opening of the National Memorial for Peace and Justice. MICHAEL P. MURPHY JR.

Michael Murphy and Patrick Weems, executive director of the Emmett Till Interpretive Center, find soil collections from central Mississippi. RICH FRIDY

Oceana Innovation Hub, St. Michael, Barbados (2024).
Iwan Baan

Second-level learning spaces at Oceana Innovation Hub, passively ventilated by fans, skylights, and operable shutters.
Iwan Baan

Students fill Oceana Innovation Hub on opening day.
Rich Fridy

Michael Murphy and artist Hank Willis Thomas stand inside 2024 Aspen Ideas Festival installation on carceral spaces.
ASPEN IDEAS FESTIVAL

The Honourable Mia Amor Mottley, S.C., M.P. and Barbados minister of education, Senator the Honourable Chad Blackman at the groundbreaking of the Chelston Climate School in Collymore Rock, St. Michael, Barbados.
RICH FRIDY

Michael P. Murphy Sr.'s last room in Barbados (photo taken in 2025).
Michael P. Murphy Jr.

Michael P. Murphy Sr. (Barbados, 2006).
Michael P. Murphy Jr.

But there was also a dark side to these shifts that's still being felt now and will be for an unknown period into our future. Cities built around offices and downtowns saw a collapse of the fragile balances of space, commerce, and culture they'd relied on. Places like New York City, Chicago, and San Francisco were shaking as they lost daily traffic to work from home, the fall of hand-to-hand commerce from workers' interactions with their surrounding environments, and the financial disruptions of businesses deciding to exit their leased workspaces

The same companies that had made San Francisco at once attractive and unreasonably expensive had also built the products that fostered the speed with which these changes took place. San Francisco's office core saw a 7 percent population decline between 2020 and 2022, and by mid-2023, more than thirty million square feet of San Francisco office space was available to rent, reflecting the wider trend of office vacancies across the country. This shift was particularly pronounced with some of the oldest and least renovated office spaces becoming obsolete.

There was an image sent around the internet of the air in Beijing, China, during the lockdown—it was clear, without the congestion and smog to which it had grown accustomed. The lagoon of Venice, famously filled with boat traffic, ship fuel, and detritus, was blue and clear. It took only a few weeks, but nature found a way to revitalize and cleanse itself.

The world was rapidly shifting the space it inhabited, and I'd now seen firsthand how heartfelt and humane these decisions around response could be and should be.

I had unknowingly prepared for this moment for over a decade. The challenge ahead wasn't just to build back—it was to rethink entirely the spaces around us as healing tools instead of those that harm us. Culture change, like nature, finds its way.

Chapter 9

THE LIGHTHOUSE

Portland, Maine

Portland, Maine, is a dynamic, small city, filled with a rejuvenating collection of top-rated restaurants, hipster bars, cocktail slingers, coffee masters, and more specialty barbershops in one downtown district than I could count in all Boston. It also has one of the largest and most concentrated collections of microbreweries on the East Coast. It feels like a neighborhood of Brooklyn packed up and colonized a smaller city on Maine's southern cost.

This was the place where I spent the bulk of the pandemic, my family and I living with my in-laws and our infant son. We then welcomed a daughter nineteen months later. Portland fills a peninsula that juts out into Casco Bay, two hours north of Boston, and looks out over a series of pine tree–covered islands that lead "Downeast"—what they call it there—to thousands of other islands that line Maine's rocky coast. It is equivalent to as much shore frontage as the entirety of the rest of the East Coast combined.

On the southern edge of Portland, the channel leads out to the mouth of the Atlantic Ocean. At the entrance to the channel, like great sentinels, stand two enormous lighthouses that bellow and radiate as beacons do, and have done for over one hundred and fifty years.

Closest to shore is Maine's oldest lighthouse, the Portland Head Light, built in 1791. It is a huge, towering exclamation point, placed at the edge of South Portland's rocky cliffs, and a tourist destination for its stunning, precarious bounty. Portland Head Light is one of dozens of other lighthouses that line the shores of Maine's coast, a testament to its maritime history and also an architecture itself, of symbolic, precarious journeys and the safe harbors beyond.

The lighthouse is a curious architecture. It says exactly what it is and what it does. It is, in a sense, pure function. It is first a light, then underneath the light, a house for the lightkeeper. The form certainly follows the function, but the lighthouse is as much a sign of what its function is—it is a beacon—as it is a built manifestation of the beacon and the infrastructural role beacons played in a maritime economy.

In the 1970s, the architecture trio Denise Scott Brown, Robert Venturi, and Steven Izenour brought their students to investigate the signifying role that architecture plays when they studied Las Vegas and its canonical sign-riddled Strip. They wanted to understand these flashy, loud buildings that emerged in the desert and were made louder by huge lit signs and thematic names. Most of the casino buildings were very similar in shape and form. They were large boxes for the casino floors, wrapped in hotel rooms above. The fundamental difference was that each had a giant ornamental sign out front delineating the façade. Their "branding."

Venturi, Scott Brown, and Izenour's conclusion was that façades are not ornamental wrappings but rather signifiers communicating information to the public about what they might desire or need. They called this "the decorated shed"—in essence a bland box store with a big neon sign saying, "Eat here!"

The contrast to the decorated shed was the notion that the

building's form derived from its function in a symbolic way. That functionality was submerged to the form itself. Their example was a building on New York's Long Island that sold ducks and duck eggs. Its form? With some humor and whimsy, it was a giant duck. The interior mattered little.

To Venturi, Scott Brown, and Izenour, the argument was that signs, decoration, and ornament should be reconsidered as valid architectural conditions to study and value. Modern architecture had pushed too far into the form-follows-function debate and had become symbolic styles themselves, and potentially elite objects, indifferent to the needs of everyday man. The decorated shed was kitsch, gaudy, and loud, but it was loved and effective, populist and potentially worthy of understanding.

The lighthouse may appear more "duck" than decorated shed. And yet, the purpose of the lighthouse is pure signal—a beacon required for safe harbor and protected passage. The architecture of the lighthouse appears somewhere in between the form-or-function debate, these theorists posited. It was not academic; it was essential infrastructure. It was a building that revealed an operating system amid us and that we relied on. The building as part of a vast system that offered life.

The nineteenth-century American poet Henry Wadsworth Longfellow grew up in Portland and regaled the Portland Head Light's iconographic position as a Prometheus beckoning to safety.

A new Prometheus, chained upon the rock,
Still grasping in his hand the fire of Jove,
It does not hear the cry, nor heed the shock,
But hails the mariner with words of love.
"Sail on!" it says, "sail on, ye stately ships!
And with your floating bridge the ocean span;

Be mine to guard this light from all eclipse,
Be yours to bring man nearer unto man!"

Today, tourists fill the park around the lighthouse and the streets of Portland. My father-in-law Kenn, who grew up there, would recount to me that it was not always this way. The Portland of his youth was rocky in another way, beat-up, when industry left the city in the 1960s and '70s. It reminded him of Poughkeepsie, he told me when we drove through it once, when the urban renewal policies came through Portland to demolish big swaths of the historic brick city in favor of car-centric parking lots and a pedestrianized mall downtown. Maybe not surprisingly, the same architect, Victor Gruen, who demolished Poughkeepsie with his team also designed the plan for Portland that demolished great swaths of the downtown core in the 1970s—including turning its iconic and beautiful train station into a strip mall.

By the pandemic, however, Portland was on an upswing, in many ways credited to restaurateurs and brewers who had settled there to create a culture of exciting and innovative food options around the abundant offerings of the seafood and agriculture of Maine's coast and land. Some parking lots had been filled in with new development, and prices were rising in real estate and attracting new buyers.

The pandemic, which forced many people to leave New York City, Chicago, and Boston, found huge resettlement in southern Maine, where people relocated for quality of life, culture, more space, natural beauty, and choice. But the restaurants, the iconographic beacons of their own culture, which were threatened, took action to counter the slow risk to their precarious bottom lines and take over the city streets.

On a date night during the pandemic, my wife and I managed to escape to the downtown district and were surprised to see it was in many ways more alive than it had been before the shutdown. The restaurants had put picnic tables and tents with heaters outside their storefronts and closed off entire blocks for pedestrian-only access. It was as if the pedestrian mall Gruen had only dreamed about had arrived just as the last vestiges of his plan were being removed by new development. People wanted to be together, safely, and restaurants banded together to remake the city and remake the roads for the public to use. It was a survival move for the restaurants to continue serving their food, but it also kept the farmers, lobstermen, vendors, and providers afloat as well.

Most of these restaurants were examples of the slow food or local food movement. They served locally harvested seafood and agriculture. Without those restaurants, the farms, farmers, and other economies were at risk.

The restaurant was just the visible and digestible manifestation of a vast economic system that was on the brink without restaurants to service it. How they shaped the city to accommodate this only revealed a deeper truth, that the places we eat link us to a broader systemic infrastructure we do not often experience. The back of house and the front of house are two dynamic worlds, and they make up the world around us. The pandemic and the move of the restaurant onto the street itself made evident and blurred this line between what was back and front, what we could see and what had been hidden from view.

Sitting along the closed-down Fore Street at a picnic table near a heater with some friends I hadn't seen in over a year, I looked around me at the highway bollards placed in parking spots and the tents and other picnic tables overtaking the road and thought the architecture was almost anti-architecture. More akin to cholera tents in Haiti than verdant, luxurious new eating establishments. Tents, sheds, decorated little booths, and temporary lean-tos were the spice of culture. It was the experience of coming together and eating that was important. The space, well, it wasn't that it was unimportant, but it was as important to be safe and secure.

I wondered about the Bilbao effect architects so proudly championed in the 1990s. Did the building influence the economic change in the city? Or rather, like here in Portland, was it the other way around, where the culture of the economic drivers shaped the built environment we felt and experienced?

Walking outside in Portland that cold spring of 2021, masking from the public, witnessing shops emptied and streets becoming filled with new signs of life, I saw architecture operating in a more elemental way. Like mushrooms growing on a decomposing tree or the sprouts of new weed growth after a fire, the built world, its elemental conditions living just beneath the surface, were revealing themselves, showing strength over what remains.

The lighthouse is not only an architecture as a symbol or beacon. It is not simply a sign but the visible manifestation of a vast network of lighthouses working together—it is what we see of the system.

The lighthouse is a theory unto itself. The lighthouse is not an architecture; it is how we see the system that is the architecture around us, shaping us, and us shaping it. To design great architecture is to reimagine the system that it serves and relies upon. It is to see the lighthouses all around us guiding us toward a better way to become an artist of systems.

―――――

The slow food movement—which was keeping Portland alive—was a good example of how a lighthouse theory transforms a vast network beneath it. Slow food is a movement contrasted to the rapid, industrialized fast-food trends of the last half century. Spearheaded by Carlo Petrini, a journalist and advocate, the method favors food that is made of local ingredients, from sustainable local farmers, and supplied by regional products from regional soils. It argues that food should be "good for us, clean in its farming practices, and fair in its labor and development."

Chefs led this movement through great restaurants. Alice Waters and her Berkeley restaurant Chez Panisse is probably the most well-known, but another is Daniel Barber and his restaurant Blue Hill, in Pocantico Hills, New York, located at the nonprofit Stone Barns Center for Food & Agriculture.

Barber had hired my team to design a master plan of the farm and agricultural center that fed the restaurant. We were engaged to help design the infrastructure that could make the system behind the slow food meal more optimized and broader, and in so doing, I learned how a real systems artist works.

————

The farm—just outside Tarrytown, New York—unfolds like a painting: cows grazing lazily on soft green slopes, rows of vegetables planted with almost military precision, and dew glistening under the early morning sun.

As I drove to my destination, the pathway deeper into the grounds twisted upward, unveiling a fortress of stone that began to emerge from the trees. The barns loomed ahead, their near-black stone walls soaring to meet slate-tiled roofs, framed by delicate wood window details. Cupolas and pyramidal chimney vents punctuate the setting like exclamation marks against the sky. Behind them, two immense silos rise, echoing the verticality of the landscape.

Built a century ago by local stonemasons, the silos seemed to grow naturally out of the land, as though they had always been there. Standing in that courtyard, I was reminded of my own ancestors— Irish stonemasons who had been brought to the Hudson Valley in the nineteenth century to construct the grand estates of a different gilded age. The parallels felt almost too perfect, as if the work of hands from the past had guided me to this moment in the present.

The Stone Barns Center for Food & Agriculture is a nonprofit dedicated to the future of farming and food systems. The heart was Blue Hill at Stone Barns, one of the world's most celebrated dining experiences, led by its chef and founder, Dan, his brother David and wife Laureen, Jack Algiere, a visionary farmer, and a brilliant crew of aspiring chefs and hospitality geniuses. He had turned this place into a crucible for rethinking what and how we eat.

Dan's tall, lanky frame was wrapped in a white chef's coat and an apron that nearly brushed the ground. He moved with purpose, his energy palpable even at a distance, reminiscent of a Brâncuși sculpture—elongated, elegant, and entirely himself.

"We're glad you're here," he said with a firm handshake.

I followed him as he toured me through the grounds from the front of house to the back to see and understand the spaces it takes to make some of the most innovative food in the world.

———

Our first stop was the mill. We walked to see where the grain is milled and bread is baked. The wafting of pure fresh bread filled the corridor. We gathered around a butcher block where a few cooks joined us.

Dan pulled a loaf off the shelf and split it open. "See the fibers? See the woven and connected tissue of this loaf? That is the gluten, binding this together. But it is a nutritious gluten, full of beneficial nutrients from the soil to the gut. Our breads are from heirloom grains we have reconstituted in a lab; these older grains are not engineered from Monsanto, and they have better flavor and nutrition and are connected to the land. The bread is not about the flour, it's about the farmer. It's about the soil," Dan told us.

At Stone Barns, they do not separate the germ from the bran, as industrial milling does, but rely on whole grain milling at Blue Hill, to ensure a rich, nutritious, flavorful loaf. Industrial agriculture stripped out the taste of the bread, they told us, but it also stripped the labor required to make local bread. Dan explained how the regional "middle tier" of wheat farmers and grain millers no longer exist, and they cannot make a regional bread revolution without creating a network ecosystem of wheat farmers and wheat millers to accompany the bread. Without them, there is no regional wheat product truly available. To reconstitute it, we need to invest in these people, these farms, and create products—great breads—where you can taste the difference. "Taste," Dan told us, "would transform the system."

This was the lighthouse again. Dan's visible experience was not a building; it was the bread at the meal, being so undeniably good that it would spark an entire ecosystem transformation, where regional wheat was once again grown. To prime the pump, however, to make it possible, those regional farms needed to be incentivized to grow the wheat and millers incentivized to open mills. To change the system, he needed great visible, tastable offerings and investments in the supply chain to keep producing them.

He was investing in the middle tier. I was struck by this concept. I recalled a similar lesson in Haiti, where it was the middle tier that was missing elements of the infrastructure. So, too, here, the system beneath us was broken and needed restitching.

Dan led us through the restaurant itself. Each product we tasted and touched had a similar story.

The restaurant was really a showroom for the farm. All this science and experimentation, testing and research was happening to create a unique meal, yes, but really it was bigger than that—it was reconstituting our food system, root to stem. To make it less fragile, to fill the particle gaps, and to restitch the fabric stronger.

This was beyond slow food. He was building a regenerative food system, and to do so was to think of every element of the system and make it the best and strongest case.

The revolution in food will come from taste, Dan told me. Taste is not as subjective as we describe it. It is hardwired into our brains from millennia of evolution, where our taste buds have evolved to sense positive and negative foods, but also depth and richness of the environment. The sense of smell is very close to the sense of taste in our brains, and so memories of smell and taste can bring us back very sharply to a specific recall from our youth or our history. As a chef, Dan embraces all the possible roles of the chef today: as food scientist, health-care provider, creative director, artistic collaborator, and experience designer. He was a systems artist. Through the story of the ingredients and the experience of sharing a meal, he envisioned a radically democratized effect, of how food systems could improve our lives.

Dan's partner, Jack, led the operations of the farm and was a co-founder of the enterprise. Jack and Dan and their team had developed a unique business model as well, outside a typical restaurant. They had multiple businesses to make this effort work. There was a nonprofit to get grants and conduct cutting-edge research. There was the for-profit to raise revenue and pay salaries. They also had farm products and seeds they were developing for distribution with venture-backed dollars to test different agricultural strands and marketplaces. They were not constrained by one market or another, but instead were seeking to change the system despite polarizing market conditions or unrealized values.

———

Dan's systems artistry was a big transformational vision. He wanted nothing less than a national reconstruction of our food system; the meal was simply his method to achieve that. Other collaborators and clients came to mind, too. I'd spent my life working on transforming systems, with Paul, with Bryan, now here, and the architecture we built was simply the physical manifestation of that dream, but the dream—the systemic change—was the real and only goal. They needed lighthouses to get to where they wanted to be.

Someone told me once that in this work, to solve the problem we needed to make it bigger. The built world was ruining our climate and hurting people around us. To reconstitute the built world around us, to serve more people, we needed something bigger than one better building of architecture. We needed to finance the systems we were working in differently. We needed a range of new business models, akin to Dan Barber's mix of businesses, that could allow us to invest in the middle tier of builders, fabricators, makers, and technicians, while allowing us to share ownership of the land with community members and finance a more environmentally regenerative building supply chain in the process. We needed the LOFAB way of building to be something more like a slow food movement for architecture. Was it possible? Could it be done?

"It definitely can. In fact, it is the only way to move architecture forward," another Dan, Dan Tangherlini, told me one afternoon on a call where I was musing about the systemic problems we were facing. We can build one building at a time through grants, but they might just make the organization more fragile unless they are returning some revenue to their bottom line and allowing them to stabilize. If we changed how we finance buildings, we could share the ownership of the land, Dan told me, and build an ecological supply chain that supports the environment instead of damages it. But he insisted that we need to build it together.

Dan Tangherlini is someone I wish my father would have met. He seems to have held all the positions my father dreamed of working in federal and city government. He was, at his core, a builder and a producer because he laid the foundational infrastructure necessary to construct entire neighborhoods. At one point he was CFO of the DC Metropolitan Police Department, the general manager of the Washington Metropolitan Area Transit Authority, city administrator in the cabinet of DC mayor Adrian Fenty, and head of the General Services Administration under Barack Obama. When I met him, he was the CFO of Emerson Collective, a foundation started by Laurene Powell Jobs, and working on a number of building initiatives, including a large housing assemblage in DC he needed to finance differently. He was also from Worcester, Massachusetts, a city not unlike Poughkeepsie in its once-thriving, then depressed, now reemerging characterization.

"We've stopped being able to build any housing, or any infrastructure, using the way we traditionally build," he said. He explained that traditional financing mechanisms were rigged and affordable housing tax credits have created a difficult marketplace to innovate in with new designs. To solve the social and environmental problems they faced in building, they have to finance their buildings differently, and do so with a more sustainable and healthy set of materials—like wood and timber and less concrete and steel. Architecture can change places, he seemed to believe, and be a beacon of change, but doing so required owning the land and sharing that ownership with the community around the structure so they can directly benefit from their community stewardship. He knew this because he had lived it, tested it, and proven it could work.

Dan introduced me to the Whitman-Walker Clinic in Washington,

DC. Whitman-Walker was a community clinic that had been on the front lines of serving the LGBTQ population before and during the HIV/AIDS epidemic of the 1980s. At the time, the 14th Street corridor was in disrepair. Much of DC had been economically shaken during the 1970s and '80s, leading to its bankruptcy and receivership in the late 1980s. Once a thriving commercial core of the Black community, 14th Street was at the time filled with empty storefronts and vacancies and was largely under-resourced. But shining lights stood out, like the Whitman-Walker Clinic, which purchased the land and set up their clinic as a direct service anchor of the community. It continued to do so for forty years.

By the time of Obama's administration in 2009, DC had come through a full resurgence. Property values skyrocketed in the district, and neighborhoods were changing rapidly. The 14th Street corridor was now thriving again and creating economic pressure to sell. Gentrification was now the critique of the neighborhood, where traditional Black owners and residents were being forced out by market pressures to wealthier and often whiter communities. Whitman-Walker was struggling with their services and financially in the red. Their one asset was their land, which they had bought forty years prior, and typically, at this stage a nonprofit will unload its assets to pay for operations. But Dan Tangherlini and some other colleagues had a different idea, which was to sell partial shares of the ownership of the land, instead of all of it. What if, he asked, Whitman-Walker became the developer of a new building, with housing above the clinic, and whose rental income would pay for the development and for the upgrade of the clinic itself? The novel idea was that he could use philanthropy as an investor instead of a grant maker, bringing in favorable investments that allowed for lower than market returns. It was a slow return strategy that shared value with those who have held the value on the street for decades, but also allowed them to modernize their asset into one that regenerates income annually. He was talking about building a bigger pool of owners.

Buildings and real estate are often blamed for extracting value and signaling change for some and dismissal of others. Some deeply want that change, but others are threatened by it if it does not include them or, worse, displaces them. This typical conversation of extraction, displacement, and removal (what gentrification's broad brush represents and is indicative of) is also at the core of architecture and its primary generator, real estate development.

And yet, growing up in a depressed city where vacancy and associated crime and commercial abandonment were the norm, I, too, heard the stories of generations of city leaders who tried to catalyze development, to create change, and to encourage investment, often to no avail. My father was one of those who tried to see significant change—and saw some but not the transformation he sought. Nevertheless, we heard how worried some community members were. They were wary of change and gentrification. There did not seem to be an easy answer. Architecture could signal positive change and also accelerate extractive real estate markets. As a nonprofit leader, I felt beholden to the community's perspective, but as an architect seeking projects, I struggled with the power relations my profession enabled and the zero-sum discussions that resulted. What power did we actually have to shift the economic conditions that underlie the market forces swirling around us. I sought to "do no harm" in our buildings but knew that after we finished the project, it was no longer in our control how it was used, or how it lasted. That is, unless we changed who owned it.

"If the community was the owner," Dan reminded me, "the risk and reward calculations would be different. Local residents would want to keep the buildings functioning well and make sure projects succeeded instead of blocking them. If the architect was the owner, she might be incentivized to make different calculations on materials and costs."

I reflected that as a nonprofit, it was difficult to be the "owner" and "investor" in revenue-generating assets. Like Dan Barber, I might need a set of complementary entities that could attract investment to create an endowment-like structure for the communities and groups I wanted to work with.

————

Dan's bigger project, however, was a new method that could also allow us to change the entire building supply chain of materials. Returning our building materials into wood, instead of more carbon-emitting materials like concrete and steel, was the fastest way to decarbonize the built world and address our own complicity in the climate crisis.

This was the other ethical dilemma I knew architects were deeply complicit in. The built environment is responsible for 40 percent of all carbon emissions. Be it the extraction of raw materials, the high-temperature curing of concrete and steel, or the delivery of materials to site, the carbon crisis was due in large part to the buildings being built the world over.

One of the newer building methodologies emerging to address climate change was actually an old one, using sustainably harvested wood and laminating it into larger beams to make structurally sound building materials. Instead of carbon emitting, trees are carbon absorbing, so wood buildings actually store carbon instead of emit it, like in concrete and steel structures. New twenty-story skyscrapers were being built with mass timber, and codes were trying to catch up.

The problem is not the forests or the wood, Dan told me. We have plenty of that. The problem is the market does not yet favor these products because the middle tier of sawmills, cut shops, CLT laminators, and builders has yet to be developed. We needed a system redesign, he told me, and we could do so by developing the buildings ourselves, financing them through community social impact grants, and reconstituting these architectures through a more robust timber supply chain to fulfill that demand. This new method would be one way to address the overlapping and systemic social, economic, and environmental crisis we face. We just needed the projects and the practices to make this happen.

Dan invited me to think about something bigger. He imagined building a movement that could jump-start large development projects in struggling cities, and to do so with unique financial strategies he and I had experience tapping for our own projects. To do that, we would need a new sustainable supply chain strategy that would own the means of production in order to share it with the communities we work in partnership with. And he wanted my help.

I could not get it out of my brain as one of the next big problems I wanted to solve. A model that could be flexible in its method of working, could tap different types of capital, and that was about changing systems instead of building buildings. I realized there was something similar to all these individuals I had journeyed and served with over the last few years. Paul Farmer, Jean Pape, Bryan Stevenson, Dan Barber, Dan Tangherlini—these were not experts in one field but multidisciplinarians, breaking boundaries between their typical practices and what change they wanted to see in the world. They were systems artists, and I wanted to build a practice that could seek out and serve the systems artists operating anywhere in the world and help them manifest their biggest, boldest ideas.

With that, I decided to set out on my next chapter of building and start a firm that could harness the multiple markets required to enact systems change. I set out to build a lighthouse.

———

Dan and his team brought me closer into his work and gave me space to launch my new practice. I received a call from one of his colleagues in the foundation and an old friend, Russlynn Ali, sharing a message from Barbados.

"I'm with the prime minister of Barbados," she began. "She wants to build a new climate science academy here." It was to be focused on oceanographic science and the rising sea levels around the islands. She wanted it built to withstand hurricanes, be climate-forward, and decolonize the educational system Barbados inherited from the British. And she wanted it done in eighteen months. "I thought you'd be the right person to help," Russlynn said.

Prime Minister Mia Mottley was a systems artist, too. She was a head of state, yes, but more so, she was an international leader advocating for restitution from wealthy nations while small countries facing the harshest effects of climate change needed a symbol of hope—something that could both anchor Barbados's future and serve as a model for other nations. She wanted a new school, but also a new way of building that would help bring jobs and opportunities to the island. She wanted a lighthouse too—a beacon of hope.

This seemed like the perfect first chance to pilot our idea outside the United States, and to get going quickly. With partners like the prime minister, Russlynn Ali, Dan Tangherlini, and the broader team at Powell Jobs' foundation, I knew we could move fast and could pilot this bigger idea, but we needed something else. Our designs needed to be replicable so that more schools could be built with the same design. They needed to be phased so that we could build now and more in the future. And they needed to be able to be rapidly deployed throughout the country with speed and without further deforesting the limited timber on the island. So we needed a LOFAB system, where materials were imported but assembled and deployed on-site. It was a challenge I could not turn down.

Now out on my own, I set about calling the best folks I knew, many of whom had gone independent in the years of COVID.

We could truly innovate and draw from our deepest wells of experience and creativity. I thought of Stone Barns again, where they had created a slice of self-sustainability by focusing on local labor and product. We would do the same here, in Barbados, and build an economic engine that supported the school construction for years to come.

We also could now build with regenerative materials like mass timber and cross-laminated timber. We could prefabricate them with sustainably harvested wood products from the Caribbean and globally so they could be deployed rapidly but train local labor in how to replicate the prototype, and we could do it so fast that it could be a model of rebuilding the world over. Finally, we could create examples like the Whitman-Walker Clinic's housing that produced income generation for future school funds and owners across the island.

A climate-forward, hurricane-resilient, sea-level-rising laboratory and school with a regenerative economic engine would be a systemic approach to solving a multiheaded problem for the future of the island and be a model for how small nations could fight the effects of change around them. This was more than a building.

A local Barbadian architect, Alyssa-Amor Gibbons, taught us about the island's architectural history, up through its post-emancipation (1834 for Barbados) era of chattel housing. Newly freed tenant farmers built small, portable wooden structures on visible blocks that could be deconstructed and moved to where the next job was. These structures allowed the farmers to own the wood and roof and floor of their homes.

In the design, these houses were masterfully clever in their simplicity. Pitched roofs, often in the shape of an "M," walls made of wooden shiplap siding covered one over the other, and the windows sat with their louvers largely open, a protection against the island's gusty, ocean-fed winds.

The free passage of wind and irregular, nonrectangular shape of the roof were devised through trial and error, though remarkably a recent study showed this kind of hexagonal-shaped home to be the ideal form for a building that can withstand our era's extreme whipping winds.

It seemed, with some modern tweaks, the chattel house was a brilliant precedent for how to build in the future.

I started thinking about a new module, one that was deployable, reconstructible, movable, and modular with a triangular roof and able to be fully open to let the wind in. Forms like hexagons kept coming to me with pyramidal roofs, lifted up on stilts to let the water through.

From my school studies, I knew the educational program had to align with the design of the school. In this condition, the teaching at the laboratory and the future school would be project based, which had seven key principles and, in ideal fashion, was configured into six triangles that, when combined, make hexagonal forms where classrooms could open up upon each other and close.

The triangle was ideal for the curriculum and the climate. I knew I had stumbled upon our form.

Now to make it real. The ideal material would be regenerative wood from sustainable forests so that we could build wood buildings again on the island, the way they used to be constructed.

Students and teachers on the ground were invited to adapt this system for building their own ideal schooling environments. The modules, each classroom triangular in form, were both uniquely appropriate for the climate and endlessly adaptable to the needs of those who would use them. The structures we landed on could be assembled and replicated on-site, and each builder could impart her or his own particular take on the structures within the structural frame. And then, ultimately, that same structure could be taken apart, moved, and rebuilt somewhere else in a matter of days in response to an ecological disaster. I felt all the lessons of the last fifteen years coming into focus.

Finally, we offered the prime minister another option, where this same module could be built into the tallest, greenest tower in the Caribbean. Using our regenerative financing, it could support a new schools fund and generate income to support ongoing maintenance and construction. It would be its own regenerative beacon of how to reconstruct the island's infrastructure from the ground up.

As we were kicking off, it took me a few conversations to admit to Russlynn that something else had come together to make this project happen. After crisscrossing the globe for fifteen years, there was something making me anxious to visit the island nation to begin the project in full. Because Barbados was where my father had chosen to die.

Chapter 10

THE LAST ROOM

Bridgetown, Barbados

had been to Barbados before with my father when he was sick, and it was a place he had visited and loved. When his time to finally succumb to cancer arrived, it was also the place he chose to die. He'd long had a plan to die in Barbados, I would later learn. He wanted to be in the company of my mother and his closest friends. A piece of me wanted to understand why my two siblings and I were not invited to be part of that final plan, but I also knew that he wanted to protect us from the worst of it. And it was hard to see.

Since his death in 2007, I had long dreamed of returning to Barbados. I wanted to trace his final steps if only to understand what motivated him and what about this place gave him the peace to let go. Russlynn Ali's call felt like a call from something bigger than me, something cosmic, asking me to walk the path of my father's last steps. If I could tap into his knowledge, maybe I could remember the reasons I had found architecture in the first place and experience the history, the spirituality, the peace that inspired him in his final days.

I was off to Barbados to begin a new journey.

I had designed a few schools in other parts of the world, but

Barbados was my first attempt at an entire school system, and I was nervous as I stepped off the plane into Bridgetown in 2024. My mother agreed to join me on this trip, as she also had not returned since Dad's passing.

As we walked through the terminal, I thought about the last time he came through here. In the years since we lost him, I had seen the world and flown well over a million miles. My mother moved slower now, releasing wafts of air as she hummed and grinned her way through a place that held such raw memories for her.

She recounted the wheelchair he was in and the awkwardness my father had felt being pushed around—he was a proud man—when he arrived at the house for his final stay.

Our rental car was soon on the way to that house, called Casuarina, the house where my parents spent their last moments together.

When we got to the house, I noticed right away how unique it was—abnormal even. It had no front door, really. It had no foyer, no coatroom. It had few walls, and it harmonically blended the interior with the outside. The openness instantly made me feel at ease. In the distance I heard my mother chatting up the two ladies who had become the home's caretakers for when guests stayed there. Mrs. Padina and Mrs. Catarina were new to the property, but an older gentleman named Bernard had been there for my father's passing. He was the groundskeeper.

Bernard had a slow gait and an immutable calmness about him, but he lit up when he saw my mother and she reacted with an endearing flood of emotion. My mother told me it was Bernard who helped my father into his chair and got him water, and who sat with him and talked about the island.

"He sat here in this chair," Bernard said. "I moved it to catch the sun on his face when he slept," he said, gesturing to the now-reupholstered seat my father found most comfortable. "Mr. Mike wanted to know about this place. He asked about the trees and the history of the island. The sugar plantations and the government. And he asked about my family."

I lowered my body into that same chair. The sight line from that spot looked out to the ocean through—as Bernard informed me—mahogany tree branches. The island had been covered with mahogany forests in the past, and most of the island's old buildings are built with this original wood, though it was now rare and would most likely be imported.

It had rained the night before, leaving small ponds on the fields beyond the house. Closer in, a vermillion lizard climbed around the interior corner of the window frame.

"We don't worry about the little things inside the house," Bernard said. A bird sat on the furniture and let out hiccups. "The monkeys, though," Bernard said. "We don't like monkeys in the house." I remembered my father telling me the monkeys were like little pests, even though back then, it sounded exotic to see one at all.

I turned my head back the way Dad must have rested his neck and looked up at the high vaulted ceiling above us. Wooden slats rhythmically lined the pitch. The deck outside snaked through other old-growth trees, a Tamarind over there with sour fruit, Shak Shak trees, named for the sound they make when the large banana-sized seeds blow in the wind, and a Casuarina tree, which the house was named after.

Bernard said he sometimes felt the presence of "Mr. Mike" in the house, especially when the sun had set. The chair moved, Bernard said, and that let him know my father's soul was there with us—living in the bardo of Barbados. "He is at peace here," Bernard said. It was like he saw the heaven he was going to while sitting here in this chair.

———

Homes on the island were designed to enjoy and protect from the elements unique to the region. Big verandas blocked direct sunlight. Heavy coral stone walls regulated the temperature, the thick walls holding on to the cool overnight air distributed it during the day, while the days' heat would similarly be released through the night.

I was still confused about how a fully open house like this one worked. I asked Bernard why it wouldn't be better to have walls closed during heavy rains and heavy winds. He explained that in a hurricane, if air has no way out of the house, it creates pressure inside and "pops" the roof off the house, destroying it in the process. Buildings that let the air through stay on the ground—which explained the open walls and open slatted windows. Even sixty years after the house was built, its unique qualities shined through the comfort of the space. They held a lesson to learn about the potential of working with, rather than against, the climate around us. Architects used to know how to build, I thought.

These careful overhangs and placement of walls and windows were its own form of technology. It had all been tuned like an instrument to make it eminently livable. There was a presence, an invisible hand of the architect who had engineered this comfort all around us.

A local book on the table informed me that the architect was named Peter Walker, who had relocated to Barbados when he married Jill Walker, a Barbadian painter and illustrator, in the 1950s. The book was of her illustrations. Walker had bought this plot of land to build their home and put down an example for other future residents to replicate. This home would be a calling card for Walker to build others like it on the island, and the house held elements that elicited strong emotional and sensory responses, like comfort and release.

Walking through a door is the clearest way to differentiate between the outdoors and the indoors, but in a house that does not have walls, the arrival sequence is more subtle and subconscious. I wondered if this is what attracted my father to this place, to have him choose it as his final resting spot.

"This is where your father asked me, as we walked into this house seventeen years ago, 'Can I finally let go?'" my mother told me. And as she sat down, she recounted their last trip here.

———

My father arrived in Barbados in mid-May 2007. He was helped out of the car upon arrival to their house, dragging his oxygen tank alongside as he entered the courtyard that linked three low, single-story buildings.

During the flight there he was barely awake, having been attached to a morphine-drip the whole way from New York. As they waited in line to board that morning, a fellow passenger looked over at the cluster of equipment with despair and side-eyed them, asking, "How long did he smoke?"

"Not once, actually," my mother snapped.

They'd driven thirty minutes north from the Grantley Adams Airport to this house, generously offered for use by a close friend, Robert Dyson, who knew my father from childhood. Dyson had given me my first grant to start MASS Design Group, and now I was in the Dyson home, swelling with emotion as the long lineage of lives impacted by his friendship became even more evident. Dyson remembered well the time five years prior to my father's death when my parents had vacationed here and fell in love with the place. He'd gifted the fateful week to my parents and their closest friends no strings attached. Dad must have known this was his last flight. "Returning would have been torture," Mom told us. "He would not have survived it."

My mother now recalled passing through the courtyard, still there, and that my father made his way across by the small wooden footbridge that spanned a pond full of bright orange koi fish. They'd walked hand to elbow, she said, shaded by a large tree that grew out of a stone outcropping next to the water as they passed through a large rectangular opening into a grand room that surrounded them with tall ceilings and soft furniture all around.

Destination finally reached, my mother breathed a sigh of relief almost large enough for the both of them. But there was an addendum, my father searching his thoughts and coming up with a question to conclude their arrival. "Can I finally let go?"

"That's why we are here," she answered. "To let go." They each might have had different ideas about what that question meant to them, and what its answer truly signaled. But he was asking her permission to die. He was fifty-five years old.

Letting go, for my father, meant settling into the comfortable chair, the one that was upholstered green and white with a soft, low saddle. It was well used, and its springs sunk deep. The ottoman aside it matched its pattern, and it rested on wheels that moved quietly over parquet floors.

Dad positioned the chair so he could look out over the veranda, with a view of a pool that was perched above an old golf course and surrounded by swaying trees. Beyond the fairway and through the branches was a peek view of the ocean. Now the vista was steady and infinite, looking west out of the Barbados coast south of Holetown, onto the Caribbean. I imagined it must have been a perfect retreat from life and, apparently, from living.

My father's friends began to show up shortly after their arrival. First, the Fredericks, Laurene and Steve, then Carol and Jeff Rossi, followed by Janet and Frank Sczelag from Chicago. They were friends from college. Then came Bobby and Sarah Rizzo, who grew up with my dad in upstate New York. They entered and gathered around him, at this spot he had chosen. Over the next few days, they kneeled beside him and filled his cup with ice chips. They told stories and drank rum punches. He read and slept, but he rarely moved from the chair except to attend to his feeding tube and colostomy bag.

The second night he was there, Dad called my cell phone. He rarely did that. I was in the middle of my finals week of the spring semester of my first year at the GSD. I was running between the studio and dinner, but I answered. "Hey, are you having fun?" I said, seemingly unaware or unable to know why he was calling. "I'll see you after my final, when you get back." "I love you, Michael," he replied, weakly. "I am proud of you." Then my phone's battery died before I could respond, and I had to run home to charge it. But he never answered when I called back.

Dad was a tall man at six feet, two inches. Most of his life he had been a bit heavier, but he wore it well, always in a suit and tie. In the last photo taken of him, he was thinner than I'd ever seen him. Probably a hundred pounds. Sweating and seated in that chair. His cancer had caused him to lose so much weight that the skin hung off his body, cape-like, and his eyes bulged as his face receded behind his cheeks. In the photo, his friends were gathered around him, standing with their hands on his shoulders.

————

Next to his chair was a pile of yellow legal pads covered in lists and checkboxes. In his sharp, angular handwriting he had been documenting the final conversations he wanted to have, his choices for people to give eulogies, the designs for his funeral, where he wanted his collection of political books to go, and detailed plans about final tasks to finish restoration of our old home in Poughkeepsie, New York. Somewhere on those same pads we would find the notes he'd made about that final trip to Barbados, along with everyone who would join him.

The yellow pages held clues about how he wanted to be

remembered and his legacy. He wanted to die comfortably, staring at the horizon, but he also wanted to leave behind as little negative impact as possible.

A friend of ours, Joe Renna, told me at Dad's funeral that he'd wished more than anything for our home in Poughkeepsie to be clear of his ghosts. He did not want bad memories of his to remain in that place for my mother or my siblings to encounter. "He did not want to haunt your home," Joe said. Whether he believed in ghosts or not, I understood the heaviness of the memory he intended to protect. And we also knew he wanted us to remember him alive. So that our home, the house we loved, would remain living as well—a stage for life after him, not a memorial of the life he'd once radiated within.

His legacy, that existential itch that lives in our waking mind, was so woven into the stone and mortar, paint and furniture of our home that he made it his last act to die far away from its foundations. He protected that house for us. It was astonishing. It was as if our home was his proof that he had existed, and within it we'd find the evidence of a meaningful legacy left behind.

Life had taught me that architecture was the business of making and designing structures. But my father seemed to want me to learn that architecture is brought to life through the stories we tell ourselves, and in the memories of the consequential acts that take place in and around the buildings we share. In this way, architecture becomes more verb than noun as it shapes us. It is a living thing.

Maybe this is why my mother later said, all things considered, that my father had "built a beautiful death." As he had built a beautiful life.

On his last day, he breathed to my mother, "You are surrounded by your closest friends. You will be taken care of." He then fell into a sleepy fog in his chair, in and out of consciousness. The friends moved him to his bed, and a few hours later he was gone. This was his last room.

My father made sure Bernard knew that he felt at peace in this house, and that he was comfortable here.

When I sat in that chair, I wondered about that. Was that a feeling only or was something else happening neurologically that my father needed to nourish by being in this place that he cherished to end his life. Was the space where he died a form of self-medication? Of palliative medicine?

A doctor named B. J. Miller would make the case that it was. Aesthetics and sensory inputs are healing to patients, he confirmed to me, and often as important as medical or scientific inputs as life fades toward the end. When I told B. J. about my father's story, he called my father's quest the search for "the Last Room." It was something not all can achieve, but to achieve it is a beautiful death.

"What would it look like," he asked me now, "if we could design the last room as we want it to be?" Could we create centers that gave people choices to die with dignity and closure? It was, of all the systems ideas I had heard, one of the most novel—and most beautiful.

Typically, in hospice care, he told me, we get one choice. One can die in the hospital or one can die at home. Homes can be complicated and leaden, and hospitals sterile and institutional. "These are not great choices," B. J. told me. Palliative health-care facilities and hospices were uncommon in many communities, and while there are some good examples, most resembled the clinical spaces families were trying to avoid.

"But what if we had a different set of choices?" he asked me. Why couldn't we design centers where our last place to live or to die was a choice we made, of the type of spaces, services, and conditions we wanted before exiting this world. It would bring such calm to so many patients and assist them as they experience and approach whatever comes after this life. It would give them peace to know these choices were available.

My father had been a lucky one to be able to, despite his early diagnosis and early death, choose the pathway he'd take out of this existence. Our home or the hospital was not how he wanted to go out. And after such a trying battle with cancer, he chose the one place he knew he could let his spirit go, far from the things he knew, far from my siblings and me, and with his wife, and best friends, and in a home looking out to the sea, comfortable and cared for. A beautiful place where he could leave the world he knew with ease.

The Last Room, Miller suggests, is not only a place we might design, but also a set of choices we could be offered to consider a more well-lived life. It is about having the choice to select places, sounds, tastes, sights, perceptions, and senses that may give us the most peace, the most wholeness. By discussing the Last Room, Miller argues, we build a vocabulary, a set of awarenesses and expectations, of the built environments and sensory experiences we want to be in for all our days, not only at the end of life. In this way, he says, facing the end is our notice to begin living today.

For Miller, aesthetic tools are essential methods to address forms of suffering in serious illness, and especially useful in the face of existential distress and experiences of meaninglessness. Aesthetics for Miller and his coauthors have the "capacity not only to diminish suffering but to actively augment aliveness," and in so doing face the fear of death by embracing a life full of awareness.

When faced with death, patients often prefer to make aesthetic choices over rational or scientific ones. Modern medical environments, Miller argues, are "anaesthetic" or devoid of design. He describes them as "more numbing—deadening—than invigorating." Palliative medicine and hospice, done well, can become that bridge between the sterile, ascetic, efficient spaces of the medical hospital and the soft, comforting, and familiar spaces of the domestic abode. Somewhere in this middle space, he states, the choices of patients at the end of life show how effective the world of perception, aesthetics, and sensory input could be in reducing harm. Many aspire to feel a sense of "wholeness" that, apparently, only aesthetic experiences can provide.

Florence Nightingale, even in her lived time of distress and disorder, argued for how important aesthetic inputs such as music, artwork, and nature were to helping patients heal and recover.

> People say the effect is only on the mind. It is no such thing
> The effect is on the body, too. Little as we know about the
> way in which we are affected by form, by color, and light, we
> do know this—that they have an actual physical effect.

————

As I sat in the soft chair where my father once sat, feeling the breeze on my skin, staring off to the horizon, listening to the sound of ocean waves while sunlight bounced all around me, I felt my senses put at ease, as neuroscientist Andrew Huberman suggested they do in all brains.

The crash of water was comforting, the winds kept my body temperature evenly cooled even though it was warm outside, and I was relaxed by the infinite line laid out in front of me between the sea and sky.

But it was something greater I felt sitting there, contemplating the totality of his and my life, the journey I'd been on since, and where these paths had overlapped. It was something bigger, a sense of awe. Susan Magsamen and Ivy Ross taught me about this feeling. "Awe is embedded in our DNA, we are literally hardwired for it," Dacher Keltner, a Berkeley professor of psychology, recounted to them. We feel it when faced with the great, immeasurable infinite things amid us, like the night sky or the trees of the forest. The brain responds, too, he claims, by slowing down, resisting analyzing, and letting go into the stillness of the moment one is in. This "peak experience" is also an experience of "transcendence," a moment when we move from an "I" to an "us" frame of mind. I could understand why he and I felt at ease.

———

When Paul Farmer dug that first fishpond I saw and we laid brick on a path and planted bushes for a medical garden deep in the Rwandan countryside, he was making the case, with his body, that the material and the natural world have healing powers; they create awe, they put us at ease and remind us to move from a sense of self to a sense of shared collective will. Like Miller, or Stevenson, or Nightingale, or Barber, or any of these systems artists I've had the fortune to serve, the point is the same, that the risk of not designing the spaces around us is far more dire, far more harmful, and far less whole than making the case to invest in the built world around us. The awesomeness we can feel from the built and natural world is literally needed for our brains to thrive.

If I look at the choices my father made to survive, like restoring his home, or to die, leaving that home unencumbered by his legacy, I begin to believe that which Bachelard posits, that the brain and our entire realm of memory are constructed through and in dialogue with the spaces around us. Making space is what makes us human.

Coda

THE STAGE

Every building has a story that is framed and reformed by the people that enter and exit through it. My father became a protagonist in a story written long ago, in a space that only came into focus sitting in that chair, staring at the sun as it set in May of 2007. The lionized Dutch architect Rem Koolhaas has said that every building has at least two lives, the one the architect intended and the one told by those who live in it afterward. My father's story ended in this house, but for me it was the beginning of a new chapter in my life, one that gave me fuel to live and a purpose to understand how these structures around us shape us and can make our lives better.

In June 2025, I boarded a flight back to Bridgetown. This time, I was not arriving for a site meeting or construction approval, I was arriving for the opening of the Oceana Climate School in downtown Bridgetown.

The school was the first of many to be built with this new methodology we designed. My new team was acting as true systems artists. We had accomplished the impossible task the prime minister inspired us to consider, a construction from foundations to completion in ten months, an otherwise unheard-of speed. The site was an abandoned piece of land on the ocean, recaptured by the government and turned into an academy for oceanographic science and climate research. The building's triangular, pyramidal roofs pooled shadows in the setting sun, and the colorful shiplap boards beamed with brightness and energy. Large openings of this all-wood, mass-timber building poured light into the classrooms, and the ocean horizon could be seen from every inch of the interior.

I watched as schoolchildren built with Legos in the open classroom and drew pictures of the facility. I stood on the balcony staring at the ocean and the horizon with my new team and partners, realizing that feeling of the impossible made possible.

A stage was set up in front of the building, and dignitaries, guests, and performers celebrated and cheered as the new school came to fruition. It was a stunning, boundless event, and it reminded me of just how comprehensive and essential a school is to a community's potential. It is the container of our future.

The prime minister invited me to present the project to the public and the cabinet and speak about its design and origin. I had been on stages for lectures and panels many times over the past fifteen years, describing the work and telling these stories. But for this talk my hands were shaking the printed sheets of paper the speech was on, and my nerves were visible on a huge digital screen showing close-ups behind me.

As I stood there on a podium, I took a breath and looked at the horizon to my left. I could not help but describe a sensation I was having, a feeling of being thrust into the future, out of my skin, at home, in a place that was not mine.

"I am at home here, in this foreign land," I started, "not because you have adopted me, but because this place is where my father found peace in his last days and where his spirit rests. I had long sought to return to Bridgetown to understand why this place and not others, why this soil, this horizon, this sunset, these buildings, these spaces inspired him or gave him the wholeness to let himself go. I wanted to understand it and now I do. I see it, all around me, a place bristling with life, of children playing, learning in the ocean, seeing in this new school the possibility of life. I saw in building this school the brightness of potential and of the hope for the future it constructed. I saw in the prime minister a dream becoming realized in protecting her country against forces foreign, domestic, and natural. I saw in my new partners a dream of new work and new impacts on education, and I saw in my new team the possibility of building new catalytic infrastructures that could jump-start new systemic overhauls. I saw systems in design and redesign, and the many artists, and architects, and agents making it happen all around me."

It was a vision I had, standing there on a podium in front of a legion of foreign leaders, sweating in the heat and the nerves of this potent moment. I saw a future clear and true. How buildings are the most evident manifestation of tomorrow, and tomorrow gives us life.

And it was then that my father's spirit seemed to lift in front of me, off the comfortable chair in the Walker house of Sandy Lane, emptied from the bardo, and floated off into the horizon, as the sun set on the western shore of Brownes Beach, of Carlisle Bay, of St. Michael's Cathedral, of Bridgetown, Barbados, in the summer of 2025. It was transcendent.

ACKNOWLEDGMENTS

This book would not have happened without the patience of so many dedicated friends, family, and colleagues. First is who this book is dedicated to, my wife and children Monique Wilde and Bobardi. To write this book was as much physical as it was emotional. Early, dark winter nights in the basement were only made possible by my family's insistence that I had the space to finish. But the toll was borne by them. To my brother, Daniel, who read every word of this manuscript and edited with clarity of voice and narrative, I am grateful beyond words. His brilliance and character are all I could ask for in a brother, and this book is as much his at is the product of our family. And too my family, I thank my mother, who, while my father gets the attention in this book, is really the heroine of this story. She has held us and our family through every valley along this long road and will remain the griot of our family. To Peter Lynch and my in-laws Kenn and Jennifer Guimond, who gave us new hope and shelter during the dark days of the pandemic, this book is also a work of your belief and encouragement.

To my editor, Nick Ciani, who picked up this book and brought the kind of editing that seems lost to history, I know this would not have existed without your thoroughness, your attention, your narrative genius, and your steady encouragement. Thank you. To the team at Simon and Schuster, Abby Mohr, Joanna Pinsker, Erin Kibby, Emma Van Deun, Abel Berriz, Alessandra Bastagli, and Susan McGrath. I'm so grateful to be working with such a team of powerful advocates.

To my agent Mark Tauber, who shepherded this project from idea to summary to realization, I thank you and your team at Watermark. They love writers and writing and brought this book to fruition. Before working with Watermark, I also owe a huge thanks to Nicholas Jahr, who fact-checked and validated every loose memory and ironed out every fuzzy recollection. He chased leads and passing references to make this book not just a recollection but a factual record of the years that made these projects happen. Thank you.

To write a book is as much about carving out the space to write as it is turning off the noise from other sources. I received a fellowship with the Emerson Collective, who provided the format and support to think about writing and summarizing this long journey—that I had long hoped I'd be able to capture in some document. They made the space for me to do it and made me do it. I loved the collegiality of so many big thinkers to actually encourage me to think bigger and bolder than I ever have. For that I have Anne Marie Burgoyne, Russlynn Ali, Daniel Tangherlini, and Laurene Powell Jobs and their wonderful teams to thank for taking me into their big nest and giving me the space to breathe, think, reflect, and produce new work. I am indebted to their patience, their love really, and the ways they support so many people and so many organizations to bring ideas into fruition in new and exciting ways.

Probably no other person at Emerson worked as hard for this book than the late Amy Low, whose death in 2024 only motivated me to finish this manuscript. She gave me some of her last days and critical attention at moments of perilous affliction, and I want to thank her family, her friends, her colleagues, and her for giving me that time amid all the other important things she needed to do. I miss her deeply, and she showed us what designing the last room could truly be about. I also need to thank Lowell Weiss, who gave me supportive enthusiasm weekly during my time as a fellow at Emerson, and to Patrick D'Arcy, Alex Simon, Kevin Dupzyk, Megan Dino, and the team at the Dial fellowship, I owe so much gratitude.

Finally to my friends and colleagues who supported and guided me through this journey, I am forever thankful. A big thank-you to John Rudikoff, who continues to be not only a reader but the truest of true friends. Friendship is about love, yes, but also loyalty, and there is no more loyal friend and colleague in my life than John Rudikoff. Thank you for being with me through every part of this journey and always providing a voice to turn to. To friends who gave early reads of this manuscript, Neel Shah, Gregory Thompson, Sam Stubblefield, Alex Grodd, and Tanya Paz, and of course, Monique Guimond, who read every word, I thank you for the attention and care you brought to the manuscript.

To the friends and colleagues and classmates, funders, and board members who helped build and champion and stabilize my first organization, MASS Design Group, into the entity that it continues to be, thank you. I am so proud of everything we were able to build and could only have done it with the belief of so many optimistic fellow travelers who have participated in building any entity driven by hope for something greater than ourselves.

To my students and colleagues at Georgia Tech and my friends and fellow architectural community, I thank you for your inspiration. And to my colleagues at AMMA, in particular Tanya Paz, Sarah Grunert, and Rich Fridy, thank you for imagining the new and building it in solidarity.

NOTES

Preface

4   *"I went to the woods because . . ."*: Henry David Thoreau, *Walden* (Norton Critical Edition: 1966), 61.

5   *"indweller"*: Henry David Thoreau, *Walden* (Norton Critical Edition: 1966), 31.

Chapter 1: The Home

15   *"What of architectural beauty I now see . . ."*: Henry David Thoreau, *Walden* (Norton Critical Edition: 1966), 31–32.

16   *"shelters daydreaming" . . . the human being's first world*: Gaston Bachelard, *The Poetics of Space* (New York: Penguin Books, 2014), 26–29.

16   *Chatterjee has found . . . aesthetics trigger pleasure receptors in our brains*: Alexander Coburn et al., "Psychological and neural responses to architectural interiors," *Cortex* vol. 126 (May 2020): 217–41, https://doi.org/10.1016/j.cortex.2020.01.009.

16   *Chatterjee has shown . . . the spaces we frequent throughout life*: Anjan Chatterjee, *The Aesthetic Brain: How We Evolved to Desire Beauty and Enjoy Art* (New York: Oxford University Press, 2014).

Chapter 2: The School

19   *The building it's headquartered in . . . decaffeinated coffee*: Krista A. Sykes, "The History of Gund Hall," Harvard University Graduate School of Design, September 17, 2024, https://www.gsd.harvard.edu/2024/09/the-history-of-gund-hall/. See also: Tom Metcalf, "Coffee Heir Became a Billionaire with an Early Bet on Invisalign," *Financial Advisor*, November 30, 2017, https://www.fa-mag.com/news/coffee-heir-became-a-billionaire-with-an-early-bet-on-invisalign-35961.html.

21   *His plans, elevations, and sections*: F. M. Simpson, *A History of Architectural Development*, vol. III (London: Longmans, Green, and Co., 1913), 104.

23   *Palladio example*: Banister Fletcher, *Andrea Palladio: His Life and Works* (London: George Bell and Sons, 1902), 62–63.

25   *"a man has no more to do with"*: Henry David Thoreau, *Walden; or, Life in the Woods* (Princeton: Princeton University Press, 1971), 60.

27 *Gehry's work was . . . an art and culture destination*: Herbert Muschamp, "The Miracle in Bilbao," *New York Times*, September 7, 1997, https://www.nytimes.com/1997/09/07/magazine/the-miracle-in-bilbao.html.

27 *an undeniable justification to the value of architecture*: William Cook, "The Bilbao Effect: How 20 Years of Gehry's Guggenheim Transformed the City," *BBC Arts*, October 16, 2017, https://www.bbc.co.uk/programmes/articles/1HL3drXNNWQVq7tpC6pMRsJ/the-bilbao-effect-how-20-years-of-gehrys-guggenheim-transformed-the-city.

28 *"It is the pervading law"*: Louis H. Sullivan, "The Tall Office Building Artistically Considered," *Lippincott's Magazine*, March 1896 (408).

33 *"Together let us desire"*: Walter Gropius, "Bauhaus Manifesto and Program," in *Modern Architectural Theory: A Historical Survey, 1673–1968*, ed. Harry Francis Mallgrave (New York: Cambridge University Press, 2005), 274–78.

36 *Studying at Gund was learning from . . . the types of spaces required to do so*: Paul Walker, *John Andrews: Architect of Uncommon Sense* (Cambridge: Harvard University Press, 2023).

Chapter 3: The Hospital

52 *Nardell pointed me to a study in Peru . . . leaking out*: Michael Murphy et. al. *The Architecture of Health* (Cooper Hewitt, Smithsonian Design Museum: 2023), 255. See also: C. J. Noakes et al., "Use of CFD Analysis in Modifying a TB Ward in Lima, Peru," *Indoor and Built Environment*, vol. 15, no. 1 (2006): 41–47, https://doi.org/10.1177/1420326X06062364. Alan Short and Sura Al-Maiyah, "Design Strategy for Low-Energy Ventilation and Cooling of Hospitals," *Building Research and Information*, vol. 37, no. 3 (2009): 264–92, https://doi.org/10.1080/09613210902885156. Kevin John Lomas and Yingchun Ji, "Resilience of Naturally Ventilated Buildings to Climate Change: Advanced Natural Ventilation and Hospital Wards," *Energy and Buildings*, vol. 41, no. 6 (June 2009): 629–53, https://doi.org/10.1016/j.enbuild.2009.01.001. A. Roderick Escombe et al., "Natural Ventilation for the Prevention of Airborne Contagion," *PLoS Medicine*, vol. 4, no. 2 (February 2007): 309–16, https://doi.org/10.1371/journal.pmed.0040068. W. Jiamjarsrangsi et al., "Inadequate Ventilation for Nosocomial Tuberculosis Prevention in Public Hospitals in Central Thailand," *International Journal of Tuberculosis and Lung Disease*, vol. 13, no. 4 (April 2009): 454–59.

52 *Nardell told me that before*: Florence Nightingale, *Notes on Hospitals*, with Evidence Given to the Royal Commissioners on the State of the Army in 1857, 2nd edition (London: Parker and Son, 1859), 25–28.

60 *Research has shown that access to an outside view*: Robert S. Ulrich, "View through a Window May Influence Recovery from Surgery," *Science* 224, no. 4647 (April 27, 1984): 420–21.

Chapter 4: The Latrine

74 *By the end, nearly 800,000 people would be infected*: Moni Basu, "Cholera death toll in Haiti rises to more than 3,000," CNN, December 31, 2010, https://edition.cnn.com/2010/WORLD/americas/12/31/haiti.cholera/index.html.

Chapter 5: The Mall

90 *a method of "Negro removal"*: James Baldwin is often quoted here in this interview with Kenneth Clark from 1963 (https://www.youtube.com/watch?v=T8Abhj17kYU), "Urban Renewal means . . . Negro Removal, that is what it means," James Baldwin, "Urban Renewal . . . Means Negro Removal. ~ James Baldwin (1963)," Vince Graham, June 3, 2015, YouTube video, 0:29, https://www.youtube.com/watch?v=T8Abhj17kYU&t=29s.

95 *In one assessment*: Malcolm Gladwell, "The Terrazzo Jungle," *The New Yorker*, March 15, 2004, www.newyorker.com/magazine/2004/03/15/the-terrazzo-jungle.

105 *Surface lots needed to be reimagined . . . to be given fresh life*: A few years later, in 2021, an article in the real estate section of the *New York Times* came out about the promise of Poughkeepsie, which suggested that the city had finally hit its stride in perception change. C. J. Hughes, "Poughkeepsie, N.Y.: A Postindustrial City Ready for Its Revival," *New York Times*, June 12, 2019, https://www.nytimes.com/2019/06/12/realestate/poughkeepsie-ny-a-postindustrial-city-ready-for-its-revival.html.

106 *A "Daylighting" movement had taken hold in other cities*: Amy Trice, *Daylighting Streams: Breathing Life Into American Rivers and Communities*, American Rivers, May 2016, https://www.americanrivers.org/wp-content/uploads/2016/05/AmericanRivers_daylighting-streams-report.pdf.

107 *Later, during the Biden administration . . . in local communities*: Vicki B. Johnson, "A Work in Progress: USDOT's Reconnecting Communities Pilot," *Planning*, September 12, 2024, https://www.planning.org/planning/2024/sep/a-work-in-progress-usdots-reconnecting-communities-pilot/.

113 *I'd read an article about a visionary*: Campbell Robertson, "History of Lynchings in the South Documents Nearly 4,000 Names," *New York Times*, February 10, 2015, https://www.nytimes.com/2015/02/10/us/history-of-lynchings-in-the-south-documents-nearly-4000-names.html.

Chapter 6: The Memorial

124 *But there are other senses . . . the vestibular and proprioceptive senses operating*: Susan Magsamen and Ivy Ross, *Your Brain on Art: How the Arts Transform Us* (New York: Random House, 2023), 47–52.

124 *Some researchers suggest . . . this hunger for "the horizon"*: Jay Appleton, *The Experience of Landscape* (London: John Wiley & Sons, 1975). Appleton's "prospect-refuge theory" proposes that humans are drawn to environments

where they can survey their surroundings (prospect) while also having spaces to hide or feel protected (refuge). See also Stephen Kaplan and Rachel Kaplan, *The Experience of Nature: A Psychological Perspective* (New York: Cambridge University Press, 1989). This book outlines the Kaplans' "preference matrix" and their information-processing theory of environmental preference, suggesting that humans favor landscapes that provide coherence, complexity, and opportunities for exploration. Roger S. Ulrich, "Aesthetic and Affective Response to Natural Environment," in *Human Behavior and Environment: Advances in Theory and Research*, vol. 6, ed. I, Altman and J. F. Wohlwill (New York: Plenum Press, 1983), 85–125. Ulrich's "stress recovery theory" suggests that humans are predisposed to respond positively to nature, arguing that natural views can reduce stress and enhance psychological well-being. Gordon H. Orians and Judith H. Heerwagen, "Evolved Responses to Landscapes," in *The Adapted Mind: Evolutionary Psychology and the Generation of Culture*, ed. J. H. Barkow, L. Cosmides, and J. Tooby (New York: Oxford University Press, 1992), 555–79. Orians and Heerwagen explore the "savanna hypothesis," proposing that humans are evolutionarily inclined to prefer landscapes resembling African savannas, which provided early humans with resources and visibility for survival. Edward O. Wilson, *Biophilia* (Cambridge: Harvard University Press, 1984). Wilson's "biophilia hypothesis" suggests that humans have an innate affinity for natural environments, rooted in evolutionary history, that enhances psychological and physical well-being.

133 *Mr. Smith is brought to a wooden dais*: Amy Louise Wood, *Lynching and Spectacle: Witnessing Racial Violence in America, 1890–1940* (Chapel Hill: University of North Carolina Press, 2009), 71–112.

134 *I learned of First Baptist Church . . . besieged by a few thousand whites who threatened to burn the church down*: Bernard Lafayette Jr., "The Siege of the Freedom Riders," *New York Times*, May 19, 2011, https://www.nytimes.com/2011/05/20/opinion/20Lafayette.html.

139 *Allen was lynched*: Equal Justice Initiative, Montgomery, AL, *Lynching in America: Confronting the Legacy of Racial Terror* (2017), https://lynchinginamerica.eji.org/report/.

Chapter 7: The Prison

143 *Vera had begun a project, Reimagining the Prison*: Ruth Delaney, Ram Subramanian, Alison Shames, and Nicholas Turner, *Reimagining Prison*, Vera Institute (New York: Oct 2018), https://www.vera.org/publications/reimagining-prison-print-report.

144 *inspired by a Norwegian government white paper*: There were two white papers written by the government: white paper 1 (White Paper no. 27 (1997–98) about NCS (hereafter "White Paper I")), and white paper 2 (https://www.regjeringen.no/no/dokumenter/stmeld-nr-37-2007-2008-/id527624/. See also Norwegian Ministry of Justice and Public

Security, *On the Norwegian Correctional Service*, April 23, 1998, accessed 15 September 2025, https://www.regjeringen.no/no/dokumenter/stmeld -nr-27-1998-/id191585. Norwegian Ministry of Justice and Public Security, *Punishment that works– less crime – safer society*, September 26, 2008, accessed September 15, 2025, https://www.regjeringen.no/no/doku menter/stmeld-nr-37-2007-2008-/id527624/.

144 *"the world's most humane" prison*: Amelia Gentleman, "Inside Halden, the most humane prison in the world," *The Guardian*, https://www.theguardian .com/society/2012/may/18/halden-most-humane-prison-in-world. See also Adams, where original quote is from William Lee Adams, "Norway Builds the World's Most Humane Prison," *Time*, May 10, 2010, https: //time.com/archive/6597005/norway-builds-the-worlds-most -humane-prison/.

145 *"That's fine for Norway"*: Veronica Horowitz, Robert Stewart, and Christopher Uggen, "Why Not Minnesota? Norway, Justice Reform, and 50-Labs Federalism," *Federal Sentencing Reporter*, vol. 31, no. 1 (October 2018): 5–13, https://www.jstor.org/stable/10.2307/26586180.

146 *"The principle of normality"*: Høidal, Are, 2018, "Normality Behind the Walls: Examples from Halden Prison," *Federal Sentencing Reporter* 31 (1): 58–66, https://doi.org/10.1525/fsr.2018.31.1.58.

146 *to make everyday life*: Høidal, "Normality Behind the Walls: Examples from Halden Prison," 64.

146 *meets the inmates and employees*: Høidal, "Normality Behind the Walls: Examples from Halden Prison," 64.

147 *aimed . . . at returning the inmate*: Høidal, "Normality behind the Walls: Examples from Halden Prison," 61.

148 *More than just a building, the Panopticon*: Jeremy Bentham, *The Works of Jeremy Bentham* (Edinburgh: W. Tait, 1843).

149 *I'd first read about the Panopticon . . . the expectations of the institutions that govern them*: Michel Foucault, *Discipline and Punish: The Birth of the Prison* (New York: Pantheon Books, 1977).

150 *"long stretches of several rows of barbed wire fences"*: Viktor E. Frankl, *Man's Search for Meaning: An Introduction to Logotherapy* (New York: Washington Square Press, 1984), 27.

151 *"If the man in the concentration camp did not struggle"*: Viktor E. Frankl, *Man's Search for Meaning: An Introduction to Logotherapy* (New York: Washington Square Press, 1984), 70.

153 *Today the San Quentin prison employs this model*: Anita Chabria, "California prison guards are dying too young. How Norway (yes, Norway) can help," *Los Angeles Times*, November 9, 2023, https://www.latimes.com /california/story/2023-11-09/how-do-you-reform-california-prisons-to -be-more-like-norway-hire-more-guards.

154 *Vast evidence shows how destructive isolation can be*: Erica Goode, "Solitary Confinement: Punished for Life," *New York Times*, August 3, 2015,

https://www.nytimes.com/2015/08/04/health/solitary-confinement
-mental-illness.html.

155 *"The average sentence"*: Høidal, "Normality Behind the Walls: Examples from Halden Prison," 60.

156 *"There's no way, with our history . . . the bodies of people who were lynched"*: Bryan Stevenson, "We Need to Talk about an Injustice," March 2012, TED, https://www.ted.com/talks/bryan_stevenson_we_need_to_talk_about _an_injustice.

157 *The others on the trip were changed*: Ruth Delaney, Ram Subramanian, Alison Shames, and Nicholas Turner, *Reimagining Prison*, Vera Institute (New York: Oct 2018), https://www.vera.org/publications/reimagining -prison-print-report.

159 *correctional officers had high rates*: Editors, "Corrections Officers: Addiction, Stressors, and Problems Faced," American Addiction Centers, January 6, 2025, https://americanaddictioncenters.org/rehab-guide/ad diction-statistics-demographics/corrections-officers.

162 *Dwayne went about finding prisons*: Reginald Dwayne Betts, "Founder's Take: 1 to 500 (and Counting!)," Freedom Reads, August 28, 2025, https: //freedomreads.org/news/blog/founder-s-take-1-to-500-and-counting.

163 *Angela Davis, whose seminal work*: Angela Y. Davis and Steve Freeman, *Are Prisons Obsolete?* (New York: Seven Stories Press, 2010).

164 *"I [do not] resent your question . . . should be asking of ourselves"*: "MASS Design Group and Freedom Reads," National Building Museum, YouTube video, 1:35:47, March 30, 2022, https://www.youtube.com/watch?v =gGfHgzhK8I8.

165 *"It should be assumed as an ultimate goal"*: Giancarlo, De Carlo, "Why/ How to Build School Buildings," *Harvard Educational Review*, vol. 39, no. 4 (December 1969): 31.

166 *"The true measure of our character"*: Bryan Stevenson, *Just Mercy: A Story of Justice and Redemption* (New York: Spiegel & Grau, 2014).

Chapter 8: The Workplace

172 *The modern office building is the apotheosis*: Historic American Buildings Survey, National Park Service, U.S. Department of the Interior, "4. EXTERIOR, GENERAL VIEW—Wainwright Building, Seventh & Chestnut Streets, Saint Louis, Independent City, MO," 1933, accessed September 14, 2025, https://www.loc.gov/resource/hhh.mo0297.photos/?sp=5.

172 *"form ever follows function"*: Louis H. Sullivan, "The Tall Office Building Artistically Considered," *Lippincott's Magazine*, March 1896, 403–9.

176 *signal the changes*: Judson MacLaury, "Government Regulation of Workers' Safety and Health, 1877–1917," U.S. Department of Labor, accessed September 3, 2025, https://www.dol.gov/general/aboutdol/history/mono-reg safepart02.

178 *a system that could adapt to any floor plan*: Nikil Saval, "The Cubicle You

Call Hell Was Designed to Set You Free," *Wired*, April 23, 2014, https: //www.wired.com/2014/04/how-offices-accidentally-became-hellish -cubicle-farms/.

178   *"Not all organizations are intelligent and progressive"*: Pagan Kennedy, "Who Made That Cubicle?," *New York Times*, June 22, 2012, https://www.ny times.com/2012/06/24/magazine/who-made-that-cubicle.html.

179   *Cal Newport's* Digital Minimalism: Cal Newport, *Choosing a Focused Life in a Noisy World* (New York: Portfolio/Penguin, 2019).

180   *"attention economy"*: Tomas Chamorro-Premuzic, "The Distraction Economy: How Technology Downgraded Attention," *The Guardian*, December 15, 2014, https://www.theguardian.com/media-network/media -network-blog/2014/dec/15/distraction-economy-technology-down graded-attention-facebook-tinder.

185   *San Francisco's office core saw a 7 percent population decline*: Maryann Jones Thompson, "It's official: A quarter million people fled the Bay Area since COVID," *San Francisco Standard*, March 31, 2023, https://sfstandard .com/2023/03/31/san-francisco-bay-area-california-population-decline -census-pandemic-covid/.

185   *more than thirty million square feet of San Francisco office space*: Roland Li, "S.F. office vacancy rate hits staggering record, with 30 million square feet empty," *San Francisco Chronicle*, September 26, 2023, https://www .sfchronicle.com/sf/article/s-f-office-vacancy-record-30-million-square -feet-18386268.php.

185   *The lagoon of Venice*: Julia Jacobo, "Venice canals are clear enough to see fish as coronavirus halts tourism in the city," ABC News, March 18, 2020, https://abcnews.go.com/International/venice-canals-clear-fish-corona virus-halts-tourism- city/story?id=69662690.

Chapter 9: The Lighthouse

187   *In the 1970s, the architecture trio*: Robert Venturi, Denise Brown Scott, and Steven Izenour, *Learning from Las Vegas* (US: MIT Press, 1972).

188   *To Venturi, Scott Brown, and Izenour*: Kurt Kohlstedt, "Lessons from Sin City: The Architecture of 'Ducks' versus 'Decorated Sheds,'" *99% Invisible*, September 26, 2016, https:/99percentinvisible.org/article/lessons -sin-city-architecture-ducks-versus-decorated-sheds/.

188   *"A new Prometheus"*: Henry Wadsworth Longfellow, "The Lighthouse," in *The Seaside and the Fireside* (Boston: Ticknor, Reed, and Fields, 1850), 123–26.

191   *The slow food movement*: Carlo Petrini, *Slow Food: The Case for Taste* (New York: Columbia University Press, 2003).

198   *Whitman-Walker was a community clinic*: Jenna Portnoy, "50 years in, Whitman-Walker builds future in underserved Southeast D.C.," *Washington Post*, March 2, 2023, https://www.washingtonpost.com/dc-md-va /2023/03/02/whitman-walker-disparities-southeast-dc/.

198   *Whitman-Walker became the developer of a new building*: Ethan Goffman, "How Whitman-Walker Health's redevelopment happened—and what it means for the nonprofit's sustainability," Greater Washington, February 22, 2023, https://ggwash.org/view/88598/how-whitman -walker-healths-redevelopment-happened-and-what-it-means-for-the -nonprofits-sustainability.

Chapter 10: The Last Room

215   *For Miller, aesthetic tools are essential methods*: B. J. Miller, J. Glaser, and J. Burke (2023), Palliative Aesthetics, in W. Breitbart & H. Chochinov (Eds.), *Handbook of Psychiatry in Palliative Medicine* (3rd ed., Oxford Academic), 339-C23.P95.

215   *Modern medical environments, Miller argues, are "anaesthetic" . . . only aesthetic experiences can provide*: Miller and team cite the philosopher Monroe Beardsley (1915–1985) to define a sense of "wholeness" that can create a "sense of integration as a person, of being restored to wholeness from distracting and disruptive influences . . . and a corresponding contentment, even through disturbing feelings, that involves self-acceptance, and self-expansion."

216   *"People say the effect is only on the mind"*: Florence Nightingale, *Notes on Nursing* (New York: Dover Publications, 1969), 59.

216   *"Awe is embedded in our DNA"*: Magsamen and Ross, *Your Brain on Art: How the Arts Transform Us*, 179.

217   *that which Bachelard posits*: Bachelard, *The Poetics of Space*, 210.

Coda: The Room

218   *The lionized Dutch architect Rem Koolhaas has said*: Rem Koolhaas, interview, "The Invention and Reinvention of the City," *Journal of International Affairs*, vol. 65, no. 2 (Spring/Summer 2012): 113–19.

INDEX

ABOUT THE AUTHOR

Michael P. Murphy is the founder and president of AMMA, a design and development collaborative focused on the ways in which space shapes our minds, bodies, and communities. In 2007, he cofounded MASS Design Group, and was president and CEO until 2022. Murphy led the design and development of its portfolio, including signature projects such as the Butaro District Hospital, the National Memorial for Peace and Justice, and the Embrace Memorial in the Boston Common. Originally from Poughkeepsie, New York, he lives in Los Angeles with his wife and two children.